CONTENTS

PREFACE

History. Hear that word and what do you think? Dull facts? Dead people? Useless dates? Forgettable events? The counterculture of the 1960's and mid-70's (the "Now" generation) essentially dismissed history. In those days, it was "eat, drink and be merry, for tomorrow we shall fry." Well, "the times, they surely are a changing!" The Holy Spirit's visit to both the Church and the street in the renewal and awakening movements of the last two decades gave some believers a taste of both the power of the Word and the world to come. A generation arose during those years who knew something of scripture and the supernatural, but had little sense of their own spiritual roots. Despite this, with strong beliefs about prophecy, they felt themselves children of the end-times, elect overcomers of the last days, and perhaps the chosen inheritors of heaven's greatest harvest. A grand and glorious vision indeed. But the great need of the Church of the 1980's is a sense of her history and destiny.

The past is full of treasure. Christians who do learn from revival history will be compelled to *want* to repeat it. You want history? Here are dates, people, facts, and events. But, if that is all you are looking for, go read something else. This book is not for you. It is not, strictly speaking, intended to be a book about *our* past at all. It is instead a record of the awesome life and deeds of Another—One who transcends our small and often shabby little human story, an Infinite Person who reaches time after time into lives just like yours and mine, making them memorable, giving them the greatness of a reflected glory.

Here, scenes from other times, other cultures, other places, may shock or surprise you; they might well be familiar scenes from your age, your time, your generation. It is living, this Gospel of revival, and it links yesterday's Bible records with tomorrow's headlines—ongoing accounts of ordinary lives being moved by an extraordinary God. He who called and empowered those mighty revivalists who changed the world before is alive forevermore. He can surely do it again.

Here, too, are sketches and excerpts from the lives and writings of people who saw God work. Some are perhaps well-known to you. And, there are those who may be strangers with even stranger experiences; still others where a little-known fact about a familiar figure may help you to see their lives or ministries in a whole new way. Is this book then about people and principles you ought to know about if you are going to get anything worthwhile done for Christ in our time? It is in part. I have listed some of the principles gleaned from past revivals where these men and women reached out in faith. But, it is so much more, because, as we said, this study is not "our" history. This is really all about

"His-story". John said it best: "This is the work of God, that ye believe on Him whom He hath sent" (John 6:29). This is the Church's too little realized past power and her present hope for survival. This, the deeds and demonstrations of the character, glory, and purity of Mighty God, is the work of *REVIVAL*.

Winkie Pratney, 1983

WHAT IS REVIVAL?

One of the problems with describing what God has done in history is that He is still alive and writing it. That reality has embarassing consequences for you and me. For one thing, He is always around to contradict our interpretations of such history. For another, history isn't finished until He steps in personally to put the final "Amen" on the whole thing.

This book focuses especially on two subjects: young people and revivals. About the only thing more written on and less understood than the subject of "Youth" is the subject of "Revival." Hopefully, this will not add to the confusion. I am, nevertheless, persuaded that revival—true revival, heaven-born, God-authorized revival—is the critical need of the hour, and the hope of this country's young. We had better understand something about this thing called revival, and know how to call on God concerning it if the bright western youth of the 1980's are going to spiritually survive and triumph in the world of the 1990's.

This is a compilation of a pretty big sweep of history. It is a sampler, if you like, of many diverse works of God from all ages and cultures. It begins in the words and records of the Bible; it traces out people and movements God uses for His glory through nearly two thousand years right up to the present time. It attempts to help you meet, even for a brief moment, some of the men and women who even now affect the Christian world. There is a great need today for such a guideline. Here, you may find people you like, people you don't, and people you never heard of all lumped together. I have not tried to make them all agree with each other on every-thing, just as you or I may not agree with everything they said or did or were. I have tried to show their strengths, as well as their weaknesses, their victories and failures, their trophies and their warts. It draws heavily on others' works, some no longer in print, but which I feel deserve to be heard by another generation. Others are more recent, and full of value; booklists are included, and I strongly encour-age you to locate the originals. If I have not included or done justice to your favorite figure, accept my apologies.

Over the past twenty years of my travels in the Western world, I have met many hundreds of thou-sands of young people. I have spoken to many of them on the subject of revival, challenged them to pray and give themselves to God for revival, and I have even been privileged to participate from time to time in some small, but real awakenings. Recently, the need for a general awakening in the West, partic-ularly in Great Britain and North America, has become critical. Yet, with so much past material available for study and so much obvious desire across the nation for revival, there is an appalling lack of understanding on the subject. For instance, if you get a chance to speak to a larger group of

Christians, try this little survey which I've used for the past 18 months:

How many of you know we *need* a revival? (Almost everyone raises their hands here. The knowledge of this fact hardly takes scholarship or devotion.)

How many of you *want* a revival? (Again, a majority opinion in church groups. And so does approximately 80% of the country according to George Gallup, Jr.)

How many of you know *what* a revival is? (The number drops off alarmingly now. Here is something we know we need, but we don't know what it is!)

How many of you have ever *experienced* a true revival? (And here, very few, if any, ever respond.) "And there arose another generation after them, which knew not the Lord, nor yet the works which He had done for Israel" (Judges 2:10). And that, friend, is the reason for this book.

Defining Revival

Webster's dictionary defines the word *revive* as a:

1. "Return, recall or recovery to *life from death* or *apparent death;* as the revival of a drowned person." Revival brings something back to life that is either now dead or seemingly dead. Revival is not for something that has never lived at all.

2. "Return or recall to *activity* from a *state of languor;* as the revival of spirits." Revival brings a holy shock to apathy and carelessness. Isaiah, call-

14

ing for God to show His manifest power says: "Oh that Thou wouldest rend the heavens, that Thou wouldest come down, that mountains might flow down at Thy presence...to make Thy name known to Thine adversaries, that the nations may tremble at Thy presence! When Thou didst terrible things which we looked not for, Thou camest down" (Isaiah 64:1-3).

3. "Recall, return or recovery from a state of *neglect, oblivion, obscurity or depression; as the* revival of letters or learning." Revival restores truth and recalls to obedience that which has been forgotten. Invariably, as either its cause or result, it is associated with reformation of doctrine and preaching.

4. "Renewed and more active attention to religion; an awakening of men to their *spiritual concerns.*" Revival accomplishes what our best spiritual efforts cannot. "Revival is necessary to counteract spiritual decline and to create spiritual momentum" (Wallis, *In The Day Of Thy Power,* p. 45). In revival, the church dormant becomes the church militant. Other Webster meanings of the word REVIVE are to "renew in the mind or memory, to recall"; "to recover from a state of neglect or depression"; "to comfort, to quicken; to refresh with joy or hope." "Wilt Thou not revive us again?" (Psalm 85:6). Revival means to reanimate, renew, awaken, reinvigorate, restore to new life that which is dying or dead; revival makes the Church whole and happy in God again.

Revival is more than big meetings, religious

15

excitement, a quickening of the saints, being filled with the Holy Spirit, or great harvests of souls. One may have one or all of these without revival. But, revival does include them all. Vance Havner defines it as "a work of God's Spirit among His own people ...what we call revival is simply New Testament Christianity, the saints getting back to normal" (Havner, *Hearts Afire,* pp. 103-104). Some think revival is only a supernatural thing of unusual events, terrifying manifestations and special times and seasons. Others view it as a steady, continuous work of God from a genuine Spirit-anointed Church functioning as it is supposed to. Both models are valid. But, often the first is needed to produce a genuine example of the second.

In the outpouring of the Holy Spirit at Pentecost, Peter declared: "This is that which was spoken by the prophet Joel in the last days" (Acts 2:16). True revival is marked by powerful and often widespread outpourings of the Spirit. Many times preaching had to cease because the hearers were prostrate or because the voice of the preacher was drowned out by cries for mercy. "The Holy Ghost *fell on* all them which heard the Word" (Acts 10:44). Jonathan Edwards' son-in-law, David Brainerd, (who prayed in the snow until it melted around him and was stained by his blood as he coughed away his life with tuberculosis), prevailed in prayer for revival among the American Indians. He describes in his journal how it finally began in 1745: "The power of God seemed to descend on the assembly 'like a rushing mighty wind' and with an astonishing energy bore all down before it. I stood amazed at the influence that seized the audience almost universally and could compare it to nothing more aptly than the irresistible force of a mighty torrent... Almost all persons of all ages were bowed down with concern together and scarce one was able to withstand the shock of astonishing operation" (Edwards, *The Life and Diary of David Brainerd,* pp. 142-143).

Revival In History

Arthur Wallis, in his classic study, *In The Day Of Thy Power,* points out that the word *revival* is determined by its usage. It had historical consistency of meaning up until recent years, where (especially in America) it began to take on a lesser, more limited sense. Nevertheless, he says, "Numerous writings on the subject preserved confirm that revival is Divine intervention in the normal course of spiritual things. It is God revealing Himself to man in awesome holiness and irresistable power. It is such a manifest working of God that human personalities are overshadowed and human programs abandoned. It is man retiring into the background because God has taken the field. It is the Lord...working in extraordinary power on saint and sinner" (Wallis, *In The Day Of Thy Power,* p. 20).

J. Edwin Orr, a prolific writer and eminent authority of both scholarship and experience on the subject, defines a spiritual awakening as *"a movement of the Holy Spirit bringing about a revival of New Testament Christianity in the Church of Christ and its related community"* (Orr, *The Eager Feet,* p. vii). It may significantly change an individual, a group of believers, a congregation, a city, a country or even eventually the world, but it accomplishes "the reviving of the Church, the awakening of the masses and the movement of uninstructed people toward the Christian faith; the revived church by many or few is moved to engage in evangelism, teaching and social action" (Orr, *The Eager Feet,* p. viii).

A. W. Tozer defined revival as that which *"changes the moral climate of a community."* Revival is essentially a manifestation of God; it has the stamp of Deity on it which even the unregenerate and uninitiated are quick to recognize. "Revival must of necessity make an impact on the community and this is one means by which we may distinguish it from the more usual operations of the Holy Spirit" (Wallis, *In The Day Of Thy Power,* p. 23).

We hear of a church posting notice of a three-day revival. This usually means a series of meetings for evangelism. It no doubt grew out of times when any protracted meetings could lead to revival and subsequent evangelism. But, we ought to distinguish between revival and effective evangelism. Revival is what the church first experiences; evangelism is then what she engages in. Revival is periodic; evangelism is continuous. "Revival and evangelism are not identical, although the word revival is frequently used to designate soul-winning efforts directed toward unbelievers. Revival will always vitalize God's people...but revival is not always welcome. For many its price is too high. There is no cheap grace in revival. It entails repudiation of self-satisfied complacency. Revival turns careless living into vital concern...exchanges self-indulgence for self-denial. Yet, revival is not a miraculous visitation falling on an unprepared people like a bolt out of the blue. It comes when God's people earnestly want revival and are willing to pay the price" ("Christianity Today," April 9, 1965).

Revival In The Bible

What *is* revival? The closest Biblical word to revival is revive or reviving from chayah (khawyaw)—"a primary root meaning to live (fig. or lit.), make alive, nourish up, preserve alive, quicken, recover, repair, restore, or be whole" (Strong's 2421.) It is used as such 14 times in the Old Testament.

One key Old Testament example summarizing this is Psalm 85:6, "Wilt Thou, *(God, the Giver of revival)* not revive us *(the need)* again *(the history of revival)* that Thy people *(the prime subjects of revival)* may rejoice *(the effect of revival)* in Thee?" *(the end and purpose of revival).* The Hebrew word is used again by the prophet Habbakuk in his heartbroken cry, "Oh Lord, revive Thy work in the midst of the years remember mercy!" (Habbakuk 3:2). Yet, revival is no magical thing. "In contrast to the ancient near east," says the *Theological Wordbook of the Old Testament,* "where men sought to link themselves with forces of life...by magical recitations...by appropriate magical rituals, in the Old Testament life is decided by a right relationship to the righteous standards of the Word of God" (Vol. 1, p. 280). That is why Charles Finney could succinctly define revival as "nothing more or less than a new beginning of obedience to the Word of God" (Finney, *Revivals of Religion,* p. 7). Revival is not magical. It is not mystical. It is, as far as men are concerned, a heartfelt return to love and faith in the living and written Word.

Dr. Wilbur Smith notes seven "outstanding revivals" in the Old Testament in addition to the one under Jonah. They include the one in Jacob's household (Genesis 35:1-15), the one under Asa (2 Chronicles 15:1-15), Jehoash (2 Kings 11;12; 2 Chronicles 23,24), Hezekiah (2 Kings 18:4-7; 2 Chronicles 29:31), Josiah (2 Kings 22,23; 2 Chronicles 34,35), the two revivals after the Exile under Zerubbabel (Ezra 5,6) in which Haggai and Zechariah play a prominent part, and finally in Nehemiah's time, in which Ezra was the outstanding figure (Nehemiah 9:9; 12:44-47).

He also summarized *nine outstanding characteristics* of these major revivals:

(1) They occurred in a day of deep moral darkness and national depression.

(2) They began in the heart of one consecrated servant of God who became the energizing power behind it, the agent used of God to quicken and lead the nation back to faith in and obedience to Him.

(3) Each revival rested on the Word of God and most were the result of preaching and proclaiming

God's law with power.

(4) All resulted in a return to the worship of Jehovah.

(5) Each witnessed the destruction of idols where they existed.

(6) In each revival, there was a recorded separation from sin.

(7) In every revival, they returned to offering blood sacrifices.

(8) Almost all recorded revivals show a restoration of great joy and gladness.

(9) Each revival was followed by a period of great national prosperity. (Fischer, *Reviving Revivals,* pp. 63-64).

The Greek equivalent of the Old Testament word for revive is only used five times in the New Testament. "Why is it not more of a New Testament word? For the simple reason that New Testament Christianity *is* revived Christianity" (Eric W. Hayden, *Spurgeon On Revival,* p. 11). This Greek word *anazao* (Strong's 326) is used for the restoration of the prodigal son (Luke 15:24,32), the resurrection of Christ (Romans 14:9), the physical resurrection of the dead in the last days (Revelation 20:5), and also for the deadly effect of sin (Romans 7:9). Evil as well as righteousness can have a "revival"; there can be an unholy uprising as well as a holy outpouring. Another equivalent New Testament word is used by Paul in 2 Timothy 1:6—"Wherefore I put thee in remembrance that you *stir up* the gift of God, which is in thee"—*anazapureo,* (Strong's 329) to "fan into flame, to revive." Some prefer to use the term "Spiritual awakening" like the promise fulfilled in Acts 2:17. This may refer to individual quickening, but revival, as we will use and define it, both includes and transcends this.

Do we want a revival? Do we really? James Burns, writing in, *Revival, Their Laws and Leaders,* said in 1909, "To the church, a revival means humiliation, a bitter knowledge of unworthiness and an open humiliating confession of sin on the part of her ministers and people. It is not the easy and glorious thing many think it to be, who imagine it filled the pews and reinstated the church in power and authority. It comes to scorch before it heals; it comes to condemn ministers and people for their unfaithful witness, for their selfish living, for their neglect of the cross, and to call them to daily renunciation, to an evangelical poverty and to a deep and daily consecration. That is why a revival has ever been unpopular with large numbers within the church. Because it says nothing to them of power such as they have learned to love, or of ease, or of success; it accuses them of sin; it tells them they are dead; it calls them to awake, to renounce the world and to follow Christ" (Burns, *Revival, Their Laws and Leaders*).

Still interested? Then, come with me—the journey begins.

PART I

The Great Reformation
1517-1560

THE GREAT REFORMATION

There were outbreaks of true revival long before the Reformation. Let's not take the time here to detail the incredible influence of some of the true Catholic saints who preceded the Reformers. Some names, of course, stand out. In the dark days of the 12th century, there was *Francis of Assisi* in his brown woolen robe with a rope belt. An ex-soldier and playboy, he had a vision of Christ "with eyes fixed on Him in tender love" that utterly freed him from his pleasure-mad ways and made him a radiant apostle of love. "His words were like fire, piercing the heart" (Fischer, *Reviving Revivals,* p. 78). Having nothing, he possessed all things. With his happy band of twelve, he was granted permission from Pope Innocent to found an order which stirred all Italy, and touched Egypt and Spain. Whole audiences responded to his challenge to forsake all and follow Jesus. The brothers eventually numbered in the thousands.

As early as the 14th century, following the Dark Ages, there were pious priests, like *Savonarola,* who soaked themselves in the Scriptures and got a prophetic word of judgment for their corrupted generation. A fasting, praying 15th century John the Baptist of his time, Savonarola's prophetic messages were fire, light, and searing conviction. Listeners paled, trembled, their "eyes glazed with terror ...tears gushed from their eyes; they beat their breasts and cried to God for mercy." One famous scholar, Pico della Mirandola said of him, "the mere sound of Savonarola's voice was as a clap of doom; a cold shiver ran through the marrow of his bones; the hairs of his head stood on end as he listened." Another tells how his sermons caused "such terror and alarm, such sobbing and tears that people passed through the streets without speaking, more dead than alive" as he prophesied coming judgment on the church and the country (Fischer, *Reviving Revivals,* pp. 84-86). Judgment came, and Savonarola became a civic leader. He continued to preach fearlessly for righteousness until a fierce reaction and opposition resulted in his ultimate arrest, torture, and hanging.

Wycliffe and *Huss* were other Reformers who heard from heaven, dared attack the religious leadership of their day and stack up all that was going on in God's name against the sacred standard of Scripture. But, it took a century more before God put His hand on the hearts of some rough-cut saints-in-the-making and used them to jolt the world out of its lip-service into a beginning of true obedience.

There were two main thrusts which brought about the Reformation. It began in Germany. With a rise in the sense of nationality, people began to resent the foreign rule of the church at Rome. They didn't like tithing to build up the Roman church dignitaries and the Roman cathedrals while their own individual churches saw little or no improvement. But, the major impetus for the Reformation was the invention of the printing press by Gutenberg in 1456. For the first time, the Scriptures were available to the masses. Upon reading the New Testament, many people became aware of the fact that the church at Rome was not strictly following the principles set forth in the Bible. This began an age of questioning and rethinking. This era was marked by the rise in men seeking reform.

Huldrych Zwingli, from Switzerland, had a weak voice, short sight, and, to put it kindly, lacked the gifts of a popular orator. Yet, his preaching set Switzerland afire (one hearer felt as if he were "lifted up by the hair and suspended in space!"). Contracts were put out on his life and he was eventually killed, cut into four pieces, and tossed into a fire.

The second Reformation leader, an earthy German named *Martin Luther,* wouldn't even shake hands with his brother Swiss reformer because he didn't like what Zwingli believed about the nature of bread and wine. Blunt, crude, rough, and often shockingly harsh in condemning people he didn't agree with, he nevertheless launched what has been called "the gigantic revolution in the history of the Christian church" (Walker, *A History Of The Christian Church,* p. 336). And, his profound experience of forgiveness in Christ gave him the courage to stand almost alone against the entire weight of established and entrenched religious deception and blow it to the winds.

The third leader, *John Calvin,* had no hand in initiating the Reformation. He thought of himself as a "quiet scholar" (his opponents thought otherwise) and was an aristocrat "practically destitute of humor or imagination." By the age of 26, he had finished the first draft of his famous work, *Institutes Of The Christian Religion*.

Here, in a little more detail, are the stories and contributions of these early pioneers out of darkness.

HULDRYCH ZWINGLI
1484-1531

Zwingli, the most rational and unsuccessful of the reformers, was born January 1, 1484, in a little gabled house in the mountain village of Wildhaus, Switzerland, the third child of a family of eight sons and two daughters. His father was a shepherd and chief magistrate of the city; his uncle the village priest. With a humanist education in Latin, music, and dialectics in Bern, he did not have a deep spiritual experience like Luther. Much of his early faith was an intellectual encounter, and he was not averse to some amorous encounters with village women. In 1519, at age 35, he moved to Zurich, assuming his new position as people's priest. Then, in 1522, following a close call with the plague and "hovering for weeks between life and death," he became overwhelmed with a sense of God's mercy and majesty. Now much more Christ-dependent, he admitted that "religion took its rise when God called a runaway man back to himself; otherwise that man would have been a desert forever." His first famous sermon, *On the Choice and Free Use of Foods,* made the eating of meat at Lent a matter of conscience, underscoring this great Reformation contribution with what Robert Dale called "the right of every man to *listen for himself* to the voice of God" (Fry and Arnold, *Reclaiming Reformation Day,* "Christianity

Today," Oct. 22, 1982, p. 36).

Zwingli was certainly not a gifted speaker; he couldn't see too well and had a soft voice. Yet, Gordon Rupp says of him, "his preaching is the secret of his dominance of the great city and not all his actions in the councils could match it. It is something with few parallels (Calvin, Knox, Latimer)— continuous Biblical expositions adjusted to the practical needs of each changing day in a community small enough for everybody to be known and where all the effective city leadership sat under the Word...scriptural preaching went on here, first of all the cities of Switzerland" (*Twenty Centuries of Great Preaching,* Vol. 2, pp. 77-91). His preaching was marked by ample scholarship, simplicity, conviction, and fervor.

Zwingli did not stop with freedom of conscience on foods. In 1523, he published his Sixty-Seven Theses, a summary of his doctrines, presenting his case for reform before the council, people, and town leaders of Zurich. In subsequent meetings, he opposed many other common church practices, including transubstantiation, papal authority, saint worship, pilgrimages, purgatory, statues, fasts, and the Mass itself. As in Luther's case, this did not help him to win friars and influence papists. Plots were made on his life; rumors spread about him.

As with Luther, some opposition to him was certainly just. His controversy with the *Anabaptists*[1]

---

[1]Anabaptists: A loosely organized group of movements which, besides practicing adult water baptism, stressed discipleship, a daily walk with Christ in love, and restoration of the Church.

over their belief in "a church of approved saints made sinless by regeneration" seemed to him, according to McNeil, "utterly unrealistic as well as unscriptural" (McNeil, *History And Character Calvinism*). He demonstrated his beliefs by authorizing the killing of them. On March 7th, 1526, the death penalty was ordered by drowning for those who practiced rebaptism. The first Anabaptist martyr to die, Felix Manz, was drowned on January 5th, 1527 while his aged mother watched from the shore. The sad thing was that most of these Anabaptists were real Christians, some with extreme views; but often just holding Christian convictions history has since proved closer to Scripture than the Reformer's own. Zwingli, like Luther, felt that complete religious freedom would lead to anarchy, and he eventually approved restrictive measures which he earlier would have considered tyrannous.

While they accomplished an amazing amount of good in God's Kingdom, the two Reformers, Zwingli and Luther, did not get along with each other. Besides this disagreement, another problem with the Reform approach was their stress on doctrine rather than character, concept rather than life. Stress on being godly was overshadowed by the stress on being right. And this tended to make the debaters forget the fruit of the Spirit in their zeal to have His truth. "To Zwingli the will of God rather than Luther's way of salvation was the central fact of theology. To Luther the Christian life was one of freedom in forgiven sonship; to Zwingli, conformity to the will of God as set forth in the Bible" (Walker,

History of the Christian Church, p. 363). In a meeting over the nature of the communion table elements, the two reformers reached no agreement; Luther refused to clasp hands with Zwingli as a brother in Christ. "To Zwingli, Luther's assertation of the physical presence of Christ was an unreasoning remnant of Catholic superstition. To Luther, Zwingli's interpretation was a sinful exaltation of reason above Scripture. Luther declared Zwingli and his supporters to be no Christians, while Zwingli declared Luther worse than the Roman champion Eck" (Walker, *History of the Christian Church,* p. 364). Disappointed, Zwingli returned to Zurich. Increasingly isolated and drawn into war, he finally lost his life. As previously mentioned, his enemies cut his body into four pieces and tossed them into a fire. But, none among the German-speaking Swiss ever attained his powerful influence.

What can we learn from Zwingli of benefit to our time? Positively, people need to hear the Word of God practically applied to life in all its aspects; Christian faith is no mere pietism but something powerful and effective in all levels of society. *Put simply, preaching can change a nation. If a Zwingli, hampered as he was by inaccurate theology, inadequate gifts, hindering legalism, and a past of shaky character, could affect the world, so can anyone. So, in the providence of God, can you and I.*

MARTIN LUTHER
1483-1548

Europe religiously and economically reached critical mass by the beginning of the 16th century. Her church was a military power, mostly hated or feared. Huge numbers of her religious leaders were blatantly hypocritical and essentially lost. The Italian clergy all supposedly took vows of lifelong poverty and chastity, but many merely paid a token church fine as regular clients in the "best little whorehouses" in Rome; they were cynical, frivolous and unbelievably flippant toward God. Even Leo, the Pope, an outwardly decent sports fan and literary man, was the object of common gossip. No expense was too great for his court festivals, amusements, theatres, and presents; his cardinals wrote him tragedies and comedies "not lacking in talent but sadly deficient in decency." Cunningham Geikie says "it was the fashion to call in question the very principles of Christianity" (Geikie, *The English Reformation,* p. 114). To pay for his parties and to finish the luxurious St. Peter's Church begun by his predecessor, Julius II, Leo spent much of his spare time asking for money, and almost any source was acceptable.

He chose the sale of indulgences, a popular, though not strictly authorized, fund-raising tool for the Roman Catholic church dating from the 11th century. Didn't Christ's infinite merits and the saints' excess good works not needed for their own salvation form an inexhaustible treasury from which the Church might draw benefits on special occasions, some suggested? (For instance, to release yourself or others out of "purgatory" pains after death.) To qualify originally, you had to go on a "Recover the Holy Lands" Crusade; later by hiring a knight for it instead; finally anyone benefitted who gave money for any purpose a Pope specified. By the time of Julius II, anyone giving (for themselves or for dead relatives) to help his St. Peter's project would surely escape church censure here and purgatory hereafter. Leo merely extended it to the rest of the world's parishes for a percentage of the profits. The Archbishop of Magdenurg, Germany, was one of many who bought in for a large sum, and then sent his own fund-raising hucksters, like Johann Tetzel, throughout Germany equipped with tricky jingles and slogans.

The light now focuses on Germany, then the drunkest nation in Europe. Her monastries were also affluent, their large holdings criticized both by the nobles who wanted them and the peasants who worked on them. The poor in general were restless, chafing at the money demanded by the local clergy. These clergymen had "acquired a vast collection of relics...a branch from the Burning Bush; three thousand particles from the holy innocents, a portrait of Christ, a 12-foot beam on which Judas supposedly hung himself, and one of the coins paid for betraying Christ.... Its value had notably increased," notes Gordon Lindsay, tongue-in-cheek, "and was now able to confer an indulgence of fourteen hundred years." They also had collected "a vast number of bones of dead saints, and had specified how much benefit was to be derived from each bone" (Lindsay, *Men Who Changed The World,* p. 63).

Yet, it was dangerous to disagree with the clerics. In the 50 years before the English Reformation began in 1517, the Spanish Iniquisition alone had burned alive thirteen thousand men, women, and children, and had racked, tortured, and thrown into fearful dungeons a hundred and seventy thousand more (Geikie, *The English Reformation,* p. 230). Humanism even then was the latest intellectual craze, unified under Reuchlin, a leader accused of heresy by the Moral Majority of his time. Advocates of the new learning looked upon this charge as an ignorant and unwarrented attack on scholarship, rallying to Reuchlin's support.

Added to this intellectual ferment were the stirrings of a popular religious awakening; people had a deepening sense of terror and concern for salvation. If this nation filled with grievances could find a bold, determined leader, his voice would have a wide hearing.

It was then that a protest against an ecclesiastical abuse "made in no unusual or spectacular fashion by a monastic professor in a recently founded and relatively inconspicuous German university on October 31, 1517" found immediate response and launched what has been called "the most gigantic revolution in the history of the Christian church" (Walker, *History Of The Christian Church,* p. 336).

Martin Luther, from whom this protest came, is one of the few men of whom it may be said that the history of the world was profoundly altered by his work. While not a great scholar, organizer, or politician, like few others, he moved men by "the power of a profound religious experience, resulting in unshakeable trust in God, in direct, immediate and personal relationship to Him, which brought a confident salvation and left no room for the elaborate hierarchical and sacramental structures of the Middle Ages" (Walker, *History Of The Christian Church,* p. 336). He equalled his countrymen in aspirations and sympathies, yet he excelled them because of his vivid, compelling faith and physical and spiritual courage of the most heroic mold.

Born November 10, 1483 in Eisleben, Luther's father was a peasant miner; his family had a simple, though stern faith in God. Mr. Luther, Sr., wanted his son to be a lawyer and entered him in a university in 1501 where Martin was known as an earnest, companionable, and music-loving student. But still, he strongly felt a deep sense of sinfulness, the ground-note of the religious revival of the age in Germany.

After graduating with an M.A. in 1505, Luther was profoundly moved both by the sudden death of a friend and a narrow escape from lightning. ("Saint Ann," he prayed, "if I survive this storm, I will become a monk!") He broke off his career, and in deep anxiety for salvation, entered a monastery for Augustinian hermits in Erfurt in July 1505. The monastery enjoyed deserved local respect under the supervision of the kindly Johann von Staupitz (1429-1503), one of the best of the mediaeval monastics. Staupitz' school made much of preaching and included some pious mystics sympathetic to Augustine and Bernard. There, Luther read one of John Huss' tracts which deeply touched him: "I wondered why a man who could write so Christianly and powerfully had been burned...I shut the book and turned away with a wounded heart" (Beard, *Martin Luther And The Reformation,* p. 165). Martin did well; he "performed the lowliest duties with a proud humility; recited prayer, froze in an unheated cubicle, fasted and scourged himself hoping to exorcize demons from his body" (Durant, *The Reformation,* p. 343). "If ever a monk got into heaven by monkery, I should have gotten there...if it had lasted longer I should have tortured myself to death" (Beard, *Martin Luther And The Reformation,* p. 156) Luther recalled later.

He survived, advanced, and the next year went to Wittenberg at the command of his superiors for a future professorship. He received his Bachelor of Theology in 1509, and was picked to go to Rome in 1510 on a mission, where he went through every pilgrim devotion possible, eventually climbing the stone steps of the Santa Scala on his bare knees. He earned so many indulgences that he almost wished his parents dead so he could deliver them from purgatory—all without any peace of heart. Rome's immorality and corruption horrified him enough to later describe it as "an abomination" where the papal court was "served at supper by six naked girls"

(Durant, *The Reformation,* p. 344). Made a Doctor of Theology in 1512, he began to study and lecture on the Bible. Though eventually made District Vicar over 11 monasteries, he still had no peace; his sense of sinfulness overwhelmed him. Staupitz helped by pointing out that true penitence began not with a fear of a punishing God but with love to God. Tauler's works also helped. Best of all, the other monks cared enough about this intense young friar to give him what was then a rare personal possession—a *Latin Bible*.

Lindsay notes: "His search of the Scriptures opened up altogether new truths to him. He saw that the whole nature of man needed to be changed. The fatalistic theology of Augustine that maintained man's destiny had already been determined, perhaps adversely, from the foundation of the world, his fate had been determined, his character fixed, and came under his scrutiny" (Lindsay, *Men Who Changed the World,* p. 64). It was a terrifying thought; it drove him back to the Scriptures. Luther gradually came to see that many of the doctrines he had been taught had no basis in Scripture. By the time he lectured on the Psalms (1513-15), he was convinced that salvation was a new relationship to God based not on any work of merit on man's part, but on absolute trust in the divine promises. A redeemed man, he thought, while still not ceasing to be a sinner, is yet fully and freely forgiven; a new life of willing conformity to God's will flows from his new, joyous relationship to God in Christ. Some scholars note that this important re-emphasis of Paul's teaching was not reformed enough; that to Paul, a Christian is primarily a renewed moral being; but to Luther he is first of all a forgiven sinner. To some it seemed that Tetzel's Roman Catholic indulgence money was to be replaced by a cheaper Protestant version. Luther, anxious to avoid works-righteousness, certainly did not help by cheerfully writing:

"Christianity is nothing but a continual exercise in feeling that you have no sin, although you sin...sin cannot detach us from Him were we to commit a thousand fornications a day, or as many murders. Is it not good news that it, when someone is full of sin, the Gospel comes and tells him; have confidence and believe...? Once the stop is pulled out, the sins are forgiven; there is nothing more to work for" (*Werke*, XL 436, XXV, 330, 142, 130).

Still Luther, like Paul, set off a spiritual H-bomb in an age of religious legality; he proved salvation was in essence a *right relationship to God*. Later, studying and speaking on the latter part of Romans, his confidence turned to conviction that godly faith gave personal assurance. From that time on, the sum of the Gospel, to him, was forgiveness of sins. It was "good news" filling the soul with peace, joy, and absolute trust in God. It was absolute dependence on the divine promises, on God's Word.

Sympathetic ears in Wittenberg listened to this new concept of salvation. Then John Tetzel (1470-1519) came near Luther's town, a polished Dominican monk with the best indulgence spiel yet. Intent on fund-raising, Tetzel painted the benefits of indulgences in the crassest terms, best seen in the proverb, "As soon as the coin in the coffer springs, the soul from purgatory's fire springs."

If Tetzel had only stayed away from Luther's turf, history would have no doubt been radically different. To Luther, now convinced that only a right personal relationship with God brought salvation, such nonsense was a declaration of war. On his Wittenburg university door, the reckless friar nailed up his "95 Theses," challenging to public debate all he found false in this and other church practices. Tetzel felt compelled to answer with his own "One Hundred and Six Anti-Theses" (December 1517), and this proved to be the spark which kindled the fire.

Luther was later joined by the brilliant young intellectual Philipp Melanchthon, a 21-year old Greek scholar in Wittenberg. Melanchthon was small, homely, frail, shy, and retiring but without equal in scholarship; when five or six hundred students daily jammed into his lectures, Luther himself sat humbly among them. Years later, Luther was able to powerfully intercede for his life-long friend who, often sick, now lay dying, eyes set, still and scarcely breathing. Deeply concerned, Luther, quoting promises of Scripture, went to prayer, and God gave him a word. Taking his friend by the hand he said, "Be of good courage Philipp, you shall not die. Trust in the Lord who is able to kill and make alive." While he was speaking, Philipp began to move, his breath came back, and he eventually fully recovered, to say, "I should have been a dead man had I not been recalled from death itself by the coming of Luther" (Lindsay, *Men Who Changed the World*, pp. 77-78).

Luther declared spiritual war with powerful tracts that set his times on fire. Contrasting his style with that of the "gardener" Melanchthon, he wrote: "I have been born to war and fight with factions and devils...I must root out stumps and stocks, cut away thorns and hedges, fill up the ditches...the rough foresters to break a path and make things ready" (Ledderhose, *Life of Philipp Melanchthon*, p. 38).

"On Good Works," published by Luther in May, 1520, not only defined "the noblest of all good works to believe in Christ" but explained that all normal trades and occupations of life were good; he denounced those who "limit good works so narrowly that they must consist in praying in church, fasting or giving alms." One of Luther's most important contributions to Protestant thought (as well as one of the most significant departures from ancient and mediaeval Christian conceptions), was to declare *natural human life* the best field of service for God rather than the unnatural limits of a monk's asceticism. "No other German author," said Will Durant, "has equalled him in clarity or force of style, in directness and pungency of phrase, in happy— sometimes hilarious—smiles, in a vocabulary rooted in the speech of the people and congenial to the national mind" (Durant, *The Reformation*, p. 368). Luther's German translation of the Bible is still the greatest prose work in the national literature; his title to leadership was confirmed in 1520 with three epoch-making works. *To The Christian Nobility of the German Nation*—written with burning conviction by a master of the German tongue—ran the length and breadth of the nation. Here, Luther argued it was no use pretending the priests were superior beings since all believers are priests. This universal priesthood meant the Pope had no exclusive right to interpret Scriptures; others than the Pope could call for a reform council; and a true free council for the reform of the Church should be summoned by temporal authorities. He spelled out programs for practical reform including cutting Papal taxes, reducing bulky government, closing brothels and theological reform in university education.

Two months later, (in scholar's Latin) his *Babylonish Captivity of the Church* attacked more teaching of the Roman church, especially sacramentalism. Later, in *On Christian Liberty*, he wrote on the paradox of Christian experience; "A Christian man is the most free lord of all, and subject to none; a Christian man is the most dutiful servant of all, and subject to every one." Free, because of Christ; a servant, because he is bound by love to conform to God's will and be helpful to his neighbor. Yet Luther's revolt was far more against Roman organization and ritual than Roman doctrine; others later would take up where he left off.

Luther had deeply rocked the boat of the Church world. The full imposing might of a papal council was called against him; they summoned him before them to Worms, demanding he recant. Terrified, some of his best friends left him. Still, Luther set his face like flint and bravely set out for the trial saying, "If there be as many devils at Worms as tiles on the roof-tops, I will enter!" (Beard, *Martin Luther And The Reformation,* p. 432). There, on that awesome day, they pointed to a row of his books; he was asked whether or not he would retract them. Faced with the combined might of his intellectual and theological peers, his courage almost failed him; he requested time to think it over. They gave him a day. Friends came to encourage him, and the next afternoon he was once more before the assembly. He acknowledged that in the heat of the controversy he had expressed himself too strongly against persons, but the substance of what he had written he could not retract, unless convinced of its wrongfulness by Scripture or adequate argument. The emperor, who could hardly believe someone would dare deny the infallibility of a general council, cut the discussion short. Eck, a chief Church official, told him (in Latin) "Martin, your plea to be heard from Scripture is the one always made by heretics. You do nothing but renew the errors of Wycliffe and Huss ...would you put your judgment above that of so many famous men and claim you know more than any of them?....I ask you, Martin—answer candidly and without distinction—do you or do you not repudiate your books and the errors they contain?" In German, Luther replied, "Unless I am convicted by the testimony of Sacred Scripture or by evident reason....my conscience is captive to the Word of

43

God. I cannot and I will not recant anything, for to go against my conscience is neither right nor safe." Then, fully prepared to die for what he believed, Luther supposedly cried out the words engraved on his memorial at Worms: "Here I stand; I can do no other. God help me. Amen" (Durant, *The Reformation*, p. 361). Proof of the highest courage, he had borne a great historic witness to the truth of his convictions before the highest tribunal of his nation. The packed audience applauded triumphantly, drowning out the authorities' hissing hatred. And, shortly after, though condemned to death by the state, Luther was abducted on the way to his sentence by the friendly King Fredrick the Wise who hid him in his castle in Wartburg. Here, in forced exile, Martin was able to finish much more writing, including Scripture translation.

What is Luther's legacy to us today? By 1517, he had given us the basic framework of Protestant theology; he had been convinced of at least three points:

(1) A man is justified by *faith alone* and not by works. (In our day, how much is made of status, power, and success in even the Christian world!)

(2) Each believer has *access to God directly*, apart from any human intermediaries. (And today, do we not feel compelled to go to our own Christian superstars for guidance instead of learning to seek God?)

(3) The *Bible* is the *supreme source of authority* for both faith and life. (A foundation not to be lightly discarded without dire spiritual consequences.)

By modern standards, Luther was certainly no saint; he was impetuous, rough, sometimes even crude. When he was angry, he issued shockingly harsh statements. Concerning the peasants' revolt, who were dangerously anarchistic in their attempts to right just grievances, Luther spoke against them, "Let everyone who can smite, slay and stab secretly or openly, remembering that nothing can be more poisonous, hurtful or devilish than a rebel....A rebel is not worth answering with arguments for he does not accept them. The answer for such a mouth is a fist that brings blood from the nose....their ears must be unbuttoned with bullets till their heads jump off their shoulders.... He who will not hear God's Word when it is spoken with kindness must listen to the headsman when he comes with his axe" (Luther, *Open Letter Concerning The Hard Book Against the Peasants*, July 1525, Works IV, p. 261).

Luther recommended execution of the Anabaptists for their excesses, advocated that all Jews be deported to Palestine, their synagogues and books burned. His attacks on the Pope were utterly unrestrained, many of them vulgar and tasteless. Yet, despite these glaring faults, many springing out of as-yet uncorrected theology and not-reformed-enough Reformation, it is still all but impossible not to like Luther. Full of faults, large in his mistakes, he loved, fought, laughed, sang, played, and wrote as a man utterly real; despite his flaws, in Christ he *lived*. His preaching, like his life, was blunt, vigorous, and creative. With songs like *"A Mighty Fortress Is Our God,"* his songwriting talents did much to put the

45

truth into the hearts of the common people. Spurgeon notes that "in Luther's day his translation of the Psalms and his chorales did more to make the Reformation popular than even his preaching; for the ploughman in the field and the housewife at the cradle would sing one of Luther's Psalms; in Wycliffe's day fresh psalms and hymns were scattered all over the land" (Spurgeon, *The Metropolitan Tabernacle Pulpit*, N3514, p. 261).

Here is a man of prodigious courage, earthy and crude, stubbornly dogmatic in debate, but a genuinely warm human being. He considered the great subject of preaching "the glory of God in Jesus Christ." In almost every sermon, he dealt with man's moral duty to act, good works growing out of inner faith, while he opposed Roman works and some extreme Anabaptist "inner light" claims. Always a common man's man, in one of his churches he preached for the "young people, children and servants of which there are more than two thousand" not the "doctors nor masters" of which there were about forty.

Luther, whose life first split a world church over truth, oddly enough died attempting personal unity for others. He became sick from over-exposure after a cold, January journey in an attempt to reconcile two friends who had quarreled. By February, it was plain he was on his death-bed. Friends gathering around him heard him quote John 3:16 and say, "Father, into Thy hands I commend my spirit; Thou hast redeemed me, Thou true God." "Do you still stand by Christ and the doctrine you preached?"

they asked. "Yes," he said. Then, with a sigh and a nod, "Who hath believed My word shall never see death." With that he fell asleep in Christ; his body is laid in the Castle Church in Wittenburg, but his works go marching on.

JOHN CALVIN
1509-1564

John Calvin had, as has been mentioned, no hand in initiating the Reformation. When he was born in 1509, Luther had already spent four agonizing years of searching; while Calvin was learning how to read, Luther was already giving evangelical lectures at Wittenberg on Romans. John was still a schoolboy when Martin publicly questioned indulgences. Yet, by 1580—only 16 years after his death—the world had been more deeply influenced by Calvin's thought than any other Reformer. His influence in "religion, theology, politics, sociology and economics goes far beyond that of any other reformer" (*TCOGP,* Vol. II, p. 134).

Sometime in 1534, Calvin experienced a "significant religious conversion"; from then to 1536, he traveled through France studying theology. And, by 1534, he had completed the first draft of *Institutes of the Christian Religion,* a lawyer's exercise in logic which he published the next year. Only 26 when he finished the last chapter of this most famous book of the Reformation, it has been called "the single most influential book on theology in church history."

What significance does this Reformer have for the twentieth century? He participated in no revivals in his time. He was no world-shaking preacher—definitely not an evangelist. He was not particularly known for his prayer life. His definition of a Christian even lacks the standard stress on being "born again." His importance is this: Calvin gave the world a picture of God's awesome power and reverence; he was the first Reformer to stress the transcendental nature of conversion. Yet, some of his followers today profess themselves in the opposite camp to those who support God's present supernatural intervention in human affairs! John's Calvinism can be summed up in one phrase, "the sovereignty of God in grace" says B. B. Warfield in *Calvin As A Theologian*. He was "pre-eminently the theologian of the Holy Spirit...It was he who first related the whole experience of salvation specifically to the working of the Holy Spirit, (he) worked it out into its details..." (Warfield, *Calvin As A Theologian*, p. 8-9). Calvin emphasized the supernatural in salvation; he supported the work of The Holy Spirit as prime witness to the Truth. "The authority of the Scripture cannot be asserted by arguments and disputations.... The authority of Scripture is to be established rather by the testimony of the Holy Spirit. For as God alone is a sufficient witness of Himself in His own Word, so the Scriptures will never gain credit in the hearts of men till they be confirmed by the internal testimony of the Spirit" (Calvin, *Institutes*, p. 30). For this reason alone, John Calvin's stress needs to be restored to our time, when we are so bound by religious rationalism, cold-hearted apologetics, and man-centered evangelism. "The central fact of Calvinism is the vision of God. Its determining principle is a zeal for divine honor"

(Doumergue, *TCOGP,* p. 143). This is the core of Calvinism—a deep sense of man's hopelessness and helplessness in the absence of God's free grace.

Another of Calvin's great contributions to the Church was the *authority and majesty of the Christian ministry*, the awesome power represented in serving an absolutely omnipotent God, who held total sway over the future of all mankind. Our age has been stripped once again of any over-arching cosmic direction; the ministry has been cynically mocked and belittled. Millions have turned to science fantasy and fiction in a hollow attempt to recapture this missing feeling of significance. This sense of destiny, of God's intervention, of history revolving not around our own little actions and doings but around God's great purposes, is a badly needed emphasis in our evangelically humanistic twentieth century church. Calvin said of the preacher:

"Let them argue with the mountains, let them rise up against the hills; in other words, be not dazzled by men but let them show that the word they carry, that is committed to them is like the royal Sceptre of God under which all creatures bow their heads and bend their knees. . . . Let them boldly dare all things and constrain all the glory, highness and power of this world to obey and to yield to the Divine Majesties; let them by this same Word have command over everyone; let them edify the house of Christ, overthrow the reign of Satan; let them lead the flock to pasture, and kill the wolves; let them bind and let loose thunder and lightning if that is their calling;

but all in God's name" (*TCOGP*, Vol. II, pp. 144-145).

We cannot really consider Calvin to be, in any sense, a "revivalist." His influence rests firmly in the Old Testament mold of reform through legal and moral means. In 1536, he met Farel who tried to persuade him to go to Geneva, an immoral, drunk city of 13,000 people. Farel's previous reform had been primarily negative, and every third house in Geneva was still a tavern. By 1555, Calvin had made two trips to Geneva. On His second visit, he gained the upper hand. With more experience in police tactics than words of knowledge, he set up a system of spies to search out moral breachments of the law. It was ultimately effective; Geneva became a model of reform, and a God-fearing city, although not, of course, an entirely God-loving one. His influence from there extended far beyond Geneva; he molded the thought and inspired the ideals of French, Dutch, and Scottish Protestants as well as the English Puritans. His ideas penetrated Poland and Hungary; before his death, Calvinism was taking root in southwestern Germany itself. "Men thought his thoughts after him. His was the only system the Reformation produced that could organize itself powerfully in the face of government hostility as in France and England. It trained strong men, confident in their election to be fellow workers with God in the accomplishment of His will, courageous to do battle, insistent on character and confident that God has given in Scripture the guide of all right human conduct and proper worship" (Walker, *History of the Christian Church,* p. 400). Calvin founded the Geneva Academy, now the University of Geneva, which became the greatest center of theological instruction in the Reformed communions. By 1564, he was seriously ill, and died on May 27.

He was a disciplined, hard worker (12-18 hours a day); he slept little, ate sparingly, fasted frequently, and amazed his friends that one man could carry so heavy and varied a burden. He had an amazing memory: he frequently preached without preparation. Beza said of his preaching, "every word weighed a pound." Taking nothing but Scripture with him to the pulpit, he supposedly preached, in one year alone, 286 sermons and gave 186 lectures on theology.

The one who thought of himself as a "quiet scholar," was (when committed to theological battle) a terrifying opponent. He called opponents "asses, pigs, riffraff, dogs, idiots, stinking beasts." They found themselves humiliated, exiled, and sometimes burned at the stake! Instead of saying, "I blame," he said, "I spit in his face." Instead of, "I am wrong," "I deserve to have my face spit upon." Instead of saying, "the Lord spurns those ceremonies," "It is as though He spat upon all those services." Instead of saying, "Perverse human nature," "each one would scratch out his neighbor's eyes" (*TCOGP,* Vol. II, p.38). An autocrat, nearly destitute of humor and imagination, he could still be a warm friend (or a warmer enemy as poor, envious, heretical Michael Servetus found out!) Servetus-Villenueve was Calvin's most embarassing *faux pas;* a famous doctor

who first discovered the circulation of the blood,
Servetus-Villenueve had a couple of odd ideas in
Calvin's time, which called down the wrath of both
Catholics and Calvinists. In his book, *The Restoration of Christianity,* published in Basel by his
brothers-in-law and intended to replace Calvinism,
Servetus-Villenueve believed Christ was not called
the Son until He was born, he had a Jewish idea of
the Trinity, and rejected the concept of infant baptism. This had already earned him two death sentences from the Inquisition; but now, he had the
unfortunate temerity to flee to Geneva, Calvin's turf.
Recognized there, he was arrested and jailed.
Finally, still disbelieving what was happening to
him, he was burned at the stake over green wood so
that it took three hours for him to die, though Calvin, to his credit, apparently suggested beheading
instead. Today, we find this as inexcuseably non-
Christian as Luther's words to the Jews, his encouraging of violent dealings with the revolting peasants,
or the Vatican executions. All we can say in Calvin's
defense is that at least he was consistent in his convictions. People in his day did what we would do
now—a cry of outrage went out through Europe,
showing that they certainly did not think, as some
sympathetic scholars have suggested, such a crime of
doctrine to be more deadly serious than a civic one.
One tract protested, "has Christ become Moloch to
demand human sacrifice?" or could we perhaps "picture Him as one of the policemen lighting the fire?"
(Verduin, *The Reformers And Their Stepchildren,*
p. 55).

Here, at heart, is one great and glaring weakness of the early Reformers. It is so often true in history that our greatest strengths are also our great weaknesses. Such essential concepts of *destiny* (election and predestination), *divine sovereignty* (a divine sense of security and purpose in history), and the *Lordship of Christ* (divine authority) became misused and extreme. Recent studies show how sometimes faulty philosophical premises were adopted by the Reformers leading them to interpret these doctrines in ways that later only hurt and embarrassed the Church. (See chapter one of Verduin, *The Reformers And Their Stepchildren.*) (Paternoster, London; 1968, Forster and Marsten, *God's Strategy in Human History,* 1973, Tyndale/Send The Light Press, Foreword by F.F. Bruce).

In ascribing all will in the Universe to God's will, in sometimes stressing Christ's Lordship to a point perilously near human irresponsibility, it was a short step to later disaster. Saying God's will created an "irresistible force" *causing* conversion led some believing "human instruments" to sometimes attempt the same thing. This had an unfortunate tendency; licensing future would-be reformers in the use of violence or civic force to accomplish purportedly spiritual ends, it gave the green light to justifying violent persecution of those deemed rebels or heretics. The sad chapters in both Protestant and Catholic histories, like the Albingensian Crusades, Spanish Armadas, St. Bartholemew Massacres, and the Inquisition fires and torture-racks, might never have been written by men who name God's name as supporter of their deeds if the Church had been more careful of her theological premises and their implications.

Some considered Calvin's economic contributions through Puritan thought to be even more significant than his theology. It eventually led to the rise of Western capitalism. Rifkin, a modern and brilliant analyst of our times, though not entirely friendly toward Calvin's contributions, points out that his ethic of work and frugality "provided the theological energy for the age of growth." He goes on to show that, ironically, capitalism has now created its own worst enemy. Puritan frugality, morality, and family structures are now the target of a system that emphasizes waste, lust, and independent individuality to survive, as materialism shifted focus from the producer to the consumer (Jeremy Rifkin, *The Emerging Order,* p. 198).

Yet, despite extremes to which our theologies can lead us, it is often possible to uphold the virtues that make one particular stress useful and God-honoring without surrendering to a compromise of our convictions. *Calvinists and Armenians*[1] have always had theological disagreements throughout history. Can we learn from our differences and concentrate on our common convictions, as this conversation between Charles Simeon and John Wesley proves?

"Pray Sir," said Simeon, (an evangelical Calvinist, to Wesley, the Armenian champion of his day)

---

[1]Calvinists: Stress God's actions alone in salvation as predestination and election. Armenians: Stress human responsibility to respond to or reject God's call.

"do you feel yourself a depraved creature, so depraved you would have never thought of turning to God if God had not first put it into your heart?"

"Yes," said the veteran Wesley, "I do indeed."

"And do you utterly despair of recommending yourself to God by anything that you can do and look for salvation solely through the blood and righteousness of Christ?"

"Yes, solely through Christ."

"But Sir, supposing you were first saved by Christ, are you not, somehow or other, to save yourself afterwards by your own works?"

"No, I must be saved by Christ from first to last."

"Allowing then that you were first turned by the grace of God are you not, in some way or other, to keep yourself by your own power?"

"No."

"What then, are you to be upheld every hour and every moment by God, as much as an infant in its mother's arms?"

"Yes, altogether."

"And is all your hope in the grace and mercy of God to preserve you unto His heavenly Kingdom?"

"Yes, I have no hope but in Him."

"Then Sir, with your leave, I will put up my dagger again; for this is all my Calvinism; this is my election, my justification by faith, my final perseverance; it is, in substance, all that I hold and as I hold it."

Two conditions of true unity are common *understanding* and common *unselfishness*. Wisdom and love—if we want revival, we need them both. It begins with each of us possessing a servant's heart and a genuine love for Christ; pianos tuned to the same tuning fork will also be tuned to one another. From such a true commitment to His Lordship, differences can be accomodated and distinctions maintained without hurtful division. Brothers in the same family may not always agree, but, they must not forget they are still brothers. Those true to Him will not hate each other. And *that*, friends, is the commonality of affection and conviction which sets the stage for His entry.

THE REFORMERS' MESSAGE

Zwingli, Luther, Calvin. From these three men and their co-workers we can derive three great truths absolutely foundational to understanding the stream of true revival. Spurgeon wrote:

"That great religious excitement has occurred apart from Gospel truth we admit; but anything which we as believers in Christ would call a revival of religion has always been attended with clear evangelical instruction upon cardinal points of truth. What was the sinew and backbone of the Reformation? Was it not clear enunciation of Gospel truths which the priesthood had withheld from the people? Justification by faith, starting like a giant from its sleep called to its slumbering fellows; and together these great doctrines wrought marvels. The Reformation was due not so much to the fact that Luther was earnest, Calvin learned, Zwingli brave, and Knox indefatigable, as to this—old truth was brought to the front and to the poor the Gospel was preached. Had it not been for the doctrines which they taught, their zeal for holiness, and their self-sacrifice, their ecclesiastical improvements would have been of no avail. The power lay not in Luther's hammer and nails, but in the truth of those theses which he fastened up in the sight of all men" (C.H. Spurgeon, *The Sword And The Trowel,* p. 216.)

George Fry and Duane Arnold in their *Christianity Today* article, "Reclaiming Reformation Day," summarize some of the Reformers' major contributions; the *recovery of Scriptures, the centrality of faith, liberty of conscience,* and the *priesthood of all believers.* In our day, these have implications in the areas of personal Bible study, personal relationship to Christ, every Christians' right and privilege to hear God's voice for themselves, and true community in believer's fellowship ("Christianity Today," Oct. 22, 1982, pp. 35-37). To crystallize what we have already explored in their lives, we can also say they gave us three great contributions:

(1) Justification By Faith—Freedom: God has chosen the ignoble things of the world to confound the privileged that no flesh should glory in His presence; the simple to confound the wise; the weak to confound the strong. He calls out of darkness into His marvelous light, from the power of Satan to the power of God, from the midst of the endless darkness to the realm of eternal light. And because He was lifted up in your place, you can go free. Bankrupt hearts need have nothing to pay. You don't have to earn a place in this holy Kingdom! Gone is all striving for merit—you can rest in Jesus and His righteousness alone. And whoever you are, whatever your vocation or position, Christ in you can make a holy calling of it.

(2) The Lordship Of Christ—Authority: The heart of a return to the authority and inspiration of Scripture is confidence in the absolute power and rulership of the One who gave it. Every Christian has

59

the right to hear God speak for himself, because every Christian can know God as their own Father. Liberty of conscience does not degenerate into immorality if we are truly ruled by the Lord Jesus Christ. It is time for renewal of zeal for God's honor! If Jesus rules the earth and He is my King, then His rulership gives me a derived authority on earth as His servant and representative.

A soldier, apparently hunting for Luther in order to arrest him, knocked on his door and asked, "Who lives here?" Luther answered, "Christ lives here!" Could you wake one night to see Satan at the foot of your bed, say, "Oh—its only you," and go back to sleep? Luther did.

(3) The Sovereignty Of God—Destiny: The power of the Christian community lies in this; we are not only members one of another because we are Blood brothers and sisters; we are also members of all people He has redeemed for Himself throughout history. This holy thing, the Church, was not invented on the West Coast last week; it is not an invention of the West, nor an innovation of recent history. We are linked indissolubly to a chain reaching back all the way to what God had in His heart before the beginning of earthly time. We are part of the essence of history, and thus have the opportunity above all others on earth to carry a high and holy sense of destiny. We are a chosen generation, a royal priesthood, a holy nation. And all power is given to Him in heaven and on earth. God can do anything He wants. The final future is not in the hands of men; the outcome of history is not limited to what we can

do and what we can concoct. God is the King of the whole Earth, and He is Lord of the Church.

But, as John Robinson, the Pilgrim fathers' pastor, reminded those who first came to the United States seeking to put these principles into practice in a nation, "many of his contempories had failed to go beyond the initial work of the first Reformers." He said, "We have come to a period in religion (when) the Lutherans cannot be drawn beyond what Luther saw. And the Calvinists stick where Calvin left them. Luther and Calvin were precious shining lights in their times, yet God did not reveal His whole will to them. I am very confident that the Lord hath yet more truth and light to break forth out of His Holy Word" (*Reclaiming Reformation Day*, p. 36).

Leaving the Reformers' contributions to their champions, their critics, and the sure mercies of God, we launch into the next great visitation of God in history the First Great Awakening.

PART II

The First Great Awakening
1700's

THE FIRST GREAT AWAKENING

The second great pattern of revival can bc clearly seen in many of the events which surrounded the next major eruption in divine destiny. Scholars have chosen to call this period "The First Great Awakening" or the "Evangelical Revival" of the 1700's, surfacing decades later in the "Second Great Awakening." Here the heroes were British and American, with a radical German thrown in for good measure. The Church had grown in grace, and this breed had less warts and more power than previously. The Puritans and the Pietists had thrown in their contributions, and now the world awaited the fire.

Our glance goes back to 1660. Dallimore describes this previous century as follows: "In the violent rejection of Puritanism that accompanied the Restoration of the English monarchy, much of the nation threw off restraint and plunged into godlessness, drunkenness, immorality and gambling. Puritans became a thorn in the side of the State church and faced increasing legal hassle. Finally in 1662 nearly 2,000 ministers—all who would not submit to an Act of Uniformity—were ejected from their churches. Forbidden to preach under severe penalties, many, like John Bunyan, imprisoned, hundreds suffered and some died. Then *Deism*[1] rose in the

---

[1]Deism: A movement of thought advocating natural religion based on human reason rather than revelation. It emphasizes morality and denies the interference of the Creator with the laws of the universe.

nation from 1660 to 1670; a vicious thought-war against supernatural Christianity, seeking to rationalize everything; the Bible, the virgin Birth, miracles. Of course the Church responded, but with coldly correct apologetics that lacked soul and fire. Large numbers, both high and low class, dropped out of the church believing Christianity to be false. Religion became ritual; the people above all feared 'enthusiasm'—anyone whose practice of Christianity showed any true fervor. Empty formality was the order of the day."

Dallimore further notes the horror of the times: "the Gin Craze began in 1689, and within a generation every sixth house became a gin shop. The poor were unspeakably wretched—over 160 crimes had the death penalty! Gin made the people what they were never before—cruel and inhuman. Hanging was a daily gala event, those jerking on the ropes were watched and applauded by men, women and children who crowded the gallows for the best view. Prisons were unimaginable nightmares; young and old, hard crook and first offender were thrown together to fight for survival. Women were treated even worse than the men; hundreds of hardened hookers and murderesses were locked into battle over scant and rotten rations with mothers caught when forced to steal to keep their children from starving. Open sewer trenches for toilets ran through the cells; hundreds jammed together in cells made to hold a score of prisoners; rats and insects everywere. One man took a dog into prison with him to help protect him against the vermin; the vermin killed the dog!" (Dallimore, *George Whitefield*, pp. 19-27).

Thus, in the decade between 1730 and 1740, life in England was morally corrupt and deeply crippled by spiritual decay. Yet, among these conditions, remarkably similar to those worldwide today, God arose in the mighty exercise of His power, which became the eighteenth century revival.

JOHN WESLEY
1703-1791

The roots of the First Great Awakening were actually in Germany, where Count Nikolaus Ludwig Von Zinzendorf, a Moravian of unlikely name, established a community called *Herrnhut* (The Lord's Watch) in 1724 and a prayer-meeting to hold it together shortly thereafter of even more unlikely duration—100 years, 24 hours a day! In this, even children wept with power before God.

These Moravians sent out two kinds of missionary teams—those to win the lost, and those to win the Church. One such bunch bumped into an unsaved English missionary. This man, born on the 17th of June, 1703, was to become one of the greatest church leaders of all time. Now 32, he was on board a ship to America. In contrast to the English, the Moravians never complained when struck or pushed and showed a "great seriousness." On January 25, 1735, a wave broke over the deck of the *Simmonds,* split the main sail in pieces, and covered the decks. "A terrible screaming began among the English. The Germans calmly sang on. The would-be English missionary asked one of them afterwards, 'Were you not afraid?' He answered, 'I thank God no.' 'But were not your women and children afraid?' 'Our women and children are not afraid to die'" (Wesley, *Journals,* p. 143).

Here are some excerpts from the Englishman's personal diary.

After landing in America, he asked a Moravian pastor, Mr. Spangenberg, advice with regard to his own conduct. "(The pastor) said, 'Do you know Jesus Christ?' I paused and said, 'I know He is the Savior of the world.' 'True,' the pastor replied, 'but do you know He has saved you?' I answered, 'I hope He has died to save me.' He added, 'Do you know yourself?' I said, 'I do.' In recollecting the event, I thought, 'But I fear they were vain words'" (Wesley, *Journals,* p. 151).

On the homeward voyage, January 24, 1738, after an utter failure in Georgia as a missionary from England, he recorded in his diary, "I went to America to convert the Indians; but oh, who shall convert me?...I have a fair summer religion; I can talk well...and believe myself while no danger is near. But let death stare me in the face and my spirit is troubled, nor can I say to die is gain." On February 1st, the day he landed, he wrote, "It is now two years and four months since I left my native country in order to teach the Georgian Indians the nature of Christianity; but what have I learned of myself in the meantime? Why, what I least suspected; that I who went to America to convert others was never myself converted to God! I am not mad, though I thus speak, but I speak the words of truth and soberness" (Wesley, *Journals,* p. 148).

Thus began the pilgrimage out of self-seeking righteousness, which went through conferences with other Moravians like Peter Bohler, and prayer and study of the Scripture, and which finally ended three months later in a little Aldersgate prayer meeting, listening to Luther's *"Preface to Romans"* on Wednesday May 24th, 1738. "About a quarter to nine, while he was describing the change which God works in the heart through faith in Christ, I felt my heart strangely warmed. I felt I did trust Christ, Christ alone for salvation; and an assurance was given me that He had taken away my sins, even mine, and saved me from the law of sin and death" (Wesley, *Journals,* pp. 475-476). That spring, he began a spiritual society at the Fetter Lane Moravian Chapel, the pattern of all later societies; that winter, he visited the Moravians in Germany and on his return began aggressive measures to evangelize in his own country, following Whitefield's example. Thus began the ministry of a man who also rose daily at 4:00 a.m., was preaching at 5:00 so working men could attend services, and who, during the next fifty-two years from 1739 to 1791, traveled 225,000 miles, mostly on horseback, and preached over 50,000 sermons. "Never," says Ryle, "did any man have so many irons in the fire at one time and yet succeed in keeping so many hot" (Ryle, *Christian Leaders Of The 18th Century,* p. 78).

His aims and objects were to give everyone something to do, make each consider his neighbor and seek his edification, call out latent talent and utilize it—in his words, to keep "all at it and always at it." In those years, traveling some 25 miles a day, he wrote 233 books on all sorts of subjects, including home health remedies (*Primitive Medicine,* in use for almost 200 years) and one of the earliest texts on electricity! A contemporary remarked that those who knew his travels wondered how he had time to write and those who knew his writings wondered how he had time to travel. "Leisure and I have taken leave of one another. I propose to be busy as long as I live, if my health is so long indulged me." "Lord let me not live to be useless," he prayed after seeing a once-active and useful man now old, enfeebled, and slow of speech (Ryle, *Christian Leaders Of The 18th Century,* p. 84).

Things the most opposite and unlike, petty and trifling, thoroughly spiritual and secular alike were mastered by his searching and indiscriminate mind, finding time for all and giving directions about all. One day, he was condensing old divinity, publishing fifty volumes of theology called the *Christian Library,* another day, writing a complete commentary on the whole Bible; another, composing hymns which live to this day. He was constantly "drawing up minute directions to his preachers, forbidding them to shout, scream and preach too long, insisting on their reading regularly lest their sermons become threadbare, requiring them not to drink spirits and charging them to get up early in the morning. Another day we find him calmly reviewing the current literature of the day and criticizing all the new books with cool and shrewd remarks as if he had nothing else to do. Like Napoleon, nothing seems too small or great for his mind to attend to; like Calvin he writes as if he had nothing to do but write, preaches as if he had nothing to do but preach and administers as if he had nothing to do but administer" (Ryle, *Christian Leaders Of The 18th Century,* p. 85).

He preached for sixty-five years, dying finally at eighty-eight, his last words were, "The best of all, God is with us" and the first words of the hymn "I'll praise my Maker while I've breath; And when my voice is lost in death; Praise shall employ my noblest powers," and at about 10:00 in the morning, "Farewell." Without a groan, he fell asleep in Christ. He left behind him 750 preachers in England and 350 in America; 76,968 Methodists in England and 57,621 in America. He, the ninth child of at least 13 children (three sons and ten daughters), his brother Charles, a songwriter, and other evangelist friends and followers would move all England, and eventually touch the world. He was, of course, John Wesley.

JOHN WESLEY'S CONTRIBUTION

Howard Snyder's research on Wesley *(The Problem of Wineskins, Community of the King, The Radical Wesley)* are important recent studies of Wesley's method, organizational skills, discipline, and community principles, as well as his reliance on spiritual power to accomplish God's work. Others point to Wesley's teachings on Christian perfection (experienced as a second blessing distinct from justification) as the major introduction of this thought into Protestant Christianity. Some Reformers, like B.B. Warfield, reared on Calvin and Luther, understandably view with horror what they perceive as extreme and choose to label as "perfection." Right or wrong, they prefer to opt for a more positional view of purity or a gradual, progressive sanctification with proper stress on man remaining fallen, though Christian. ("We sin every day in thought, word, and deed.")

Criticism, sometimes in reaction to what is correctly seen as a departure from Reform tradition, has been leveled at Wesley's teaching on perfection, from those who trace all second-blessing, holiness, Keswick, Pentecostal and charismatic movements to Wesley's teachings. Whether Wesley and his followers departed from Scripture as well is quite another matter. Still, it is true (as we shall later see) that Finney, Mahan, Caughy, and Walter and Phoebe Palmer, who preached a modified Weslyan doctrine of Christian perfection, almost dominated American revivalism for thirty years. Their work, especially that of the Palmer's, was especially important to the revival of 1857-58. Wesley's work, carried on by others, significantly affected the the theology of American churches, moving them away from their earlier roots, often for the better, though sometimes too far. These Holiness evangelists spread this "layman's revival" to Europe in the beginning of the "Second Evangelical Awakening." We will consider their message later.

When Wesley was still at college in 1732, "Fogs Weekly Journal" had the dubious distinction of being the first to publicly criticize him. William Law defended him in a way that turned out to be prophetic:

"It looks as if the strict rule of primitive Christianity is removed a great way out of sight, that we are not able to behold the attempt to revise it without wonder and offense. If it shall please God to give these gentlemen the grace to persevere and the blessing of so long a life, they may be the means of reforming a vicious world; and may rejoice at the good they have done perhaps half a century after most of their social opponents, the gay scoffers of the present generation are laid low and forgotten as if they had never been" (Garth Lean, *Strangely Warmed,* p. 28-30).

Let's look at the heritage which produced such an influential man used mightily of God.

JOHN WESLEY'S PARENTS

What are the parents of a world changer like? What happens when a man or woman of God seeks Him faithfully only to be apparently disappointed in his own lifetime? And, how much can a mother and a father do to instill in a child a sense of divine destiny and a desire to affect his generation for Christ? From A. T. Quiller-Couch's rare biography of Wesley's sister, Hetty, comes a beautiful and moving account of Samuel and Suzanna, the parents of England's great revival team, John and Charles Wesley.

"He was of a lean, wiry build; his nose and eyes announced obstinacy; his eyes, quick and fiery, warned you he was of the aggressive kind that not only holds on to his purpose but never ceases nagging until it be attained. And his carriage was amazingly dignified for one who, to be precise, stood but five feet five and a half inches high."

Samuel Wesley had been a non-juring clergyman, one of the many whose livelihood was eliminated on St. Bartholomew's day, 1662. He himself had been educated as a non-conformist at Mr. Morton's famous academy on Newington Green where Daniel Defoe had proceeded him as a pupil, and where he had heard John Bunyan preach. Tracts leveled against the Dissenters that he was supposed to answer and defend had the opposite effect; he renounced Dissent instead and attached himself to the Established church! He lived with his mother and an old aunt, themselves ardent Dissenters who were unaware of his design. One morning before daybreak, in 1683, he set out to enter Oxford as a poor student with only 45 shillings in his pocket.

For the five years he studied at Oxford, he received only five shillings from his family and friends. To support himself, he instructed wealthier undergraduates, writing their exercises for them, and as a servitor had to black their boots and run their errands. With all this, he found the time and the will to be charitable and visit the prisoners in the Castle at Oxford, many imprisoned for debts. He finally earned his Bachelor's degree, and left the University seventeen pounds and fifteen shillings richer than when he had entered. Dunton, a brother, had married Elizabeth, one of the many daughters of Dr. Samuel Annesly, the famous Dissenter. As a student at Newington Green, Samuel Wesley was present at the wedding and met Suzanna, the doctor's youngest daughter, then a slight girl of 14. Also secretly thinking the Church to be right and her father wrong, she felt herself an alien in her own house. So it happened that Samuel, halting awkwardly before this slip of a girl and stammering some words meant to comfort her for losing her sister, found himself answering strange questions. He stared into young eyes which had somehow surprised his own doubts of Dissent and beyond them into a mind which had come to its own decision and quietly, firmly invited him to follow. It startled him so much that love dawned at the same moment with a lesser shock. He seated himself on the window cushion beside her; after this they talked very little but watched the guests, feeling like two conspirators in the crowd. Thus it was that Sam dropped his pen, packed his books, and tramped off to Oxford. After coming home and being appointed chaplain on a man-of-war, his income rose enough to marry Suzanna, now 20, in 1689.

Less than a year later, their first child, Samuel, was born; they moved to South Ormsby on Mid-summer Day, 1690, to a vicarage little better than a mud hut until the spring of 1697 where Suzanna bore Emilia, Susannah, and Molly besides other children who died in infancy.

Wesley was chaplain to the Marquis of Nomandy (who invited them down); he was arrogantly immoral, and he and his mistresses gave Sam much searching of heart. Because Sam ushered out a hooker who took a liking to his wife, Sam lost his job and moved to Epworth. There, his new parishioners hated his politics and made life for him as miserable as they could. They were savage fighters, but in him they met their match. In 1702, they set fire secretly to the parsonage and burnt two-thirds of it down. In the winter of 1704, they destroyed a great part of his flax crop.

The Dissenters looked on him as the worst of foes—one who had left their own ranks.

Wesley remarks on his position at that time: "I went to Lincoln on Tuesday night and the election (Tory members lost to Whig candidates which Dissenters supported) began Wednesday the 30th. A great part of the night our Isle people kept drumming and shouting and firing pistols and guns under the windows where my wife lay who had been brought to bed not three weeks. I had put the child to nurse over against my own house; the noise kept his nurse waking till one or two in the morning. Then they left off and the nurse heavy with sleep overlaid the child. She woke, found it dead, ran it over to my house almost distracted, and calling my servants, threw it into their arms. They as wise as she ran up with it to my wife, and before she was well awake, threw it cold and dead into hers. She composed herself as well as she could and that day got it buried. A clergyman met me in the yard and told me to withdraw for the Isle men intended me a mischief. Another said he had heard 20 men say, 'if they got me in the castle yard they would squeeze my guts out.' I went by Gainsboro and God preserved me. When they knew I was home, they sent the drum and mob with guns etc. as usual to compliment me till after midnight. One of them passing by Friday evening and seeing my children in the yard cried out, 'O ye devils! We will come and turn ye all out of doors a-begging shortly.' God convert them and forgive them. All this, thank God does not in the least sink my wife's spirits. For my own, I feel disturbed and disordered."

"Blessed are ye, when men shall revile you."

Sam was betrayed by a servant, and thrown into prison for a thirty pound debt he could not pay for losing his regiment and crop. "I thank God my wife was pretty well recovered and churched some days before I was taken from her. And hope she'll be able to look to my family, if they don't turn them out of doors as they have often threatened to do. One of my biggest concerns was my being forced to leave my poor lambs in the middle of so many wolves. But the great Shepherd is able to provide for them and to preserve them. My wife bears it with a courage which becomes her and which I expected from her."

They stabbed his cows to dry up their milk, hoping to starve his family; they tore the latch of the door in order to shoot back the lock "which nobody will think was with intention to rob my family. . . . My house dog, who made a huge noise within doors was sufficiently punished for his wants of politics and moderation, for the next day his leg was almost chopped off by an unknown hand. 'Tis not every one that could bear things; but I bless God my wife is less concerned with suffering them than I am in the writing. . . . Oh my Lord. I once more repeat it, that I shall at some time have a more equal Judge than any in this world. Most of my friends advise me to leave Epworth if I should ever get from hence. I confess I am not of that mind because I may yet do good there; and 'tis like a coward to desert my post because the enemy fire thick upon me. They have only wounded me yet, and I believe *can't* kill me. I hope to be home by Christmas. God help my poor family!"

By the end of the year (the Archbishop and friends assisting), he was home and refused to budge from

Epworth. For over three years the rage of his enemies slumbered and his affairs grew easier. John (if we don't count the poor child who had been overlaid), had been the last child born before Sam's imprisonment. Then, Patty arrived in the autumn of 1706, and Charles in December 1707. A third was expected when, on the night of February 9th, 1709, the parsonage took fire again and burned to the ground in 15 minutes.

"A branch plucked from the burning."

Here, in Sam Wesley's words, is an account of the awful event which was to precipitate in John Wesley's heart the desire to change the world:

"I ran down and went to my children in the garden to help them over the wall. When I was without, I heard one of my poor lambs left still above stairs about six years old cry out dismally 'Help me!' I ran in again, to go upstairs, but the staircase was now all afire. I tried to force up through it a second time holding my breeches over my head, but the stream of fire beat me down. I thought I had done my duty; went out of the house to that part of my family I had saved, with the killing cry of my child in my ears. I made them all kneel down and we prayed to God to receive his soul.

"I tried to break down the pales and get my children over into the street but could not; they went under the flame and got over the wall. Now I put on my breeches and leaped after them. One of my maidservants that had brought out the least child got out much at the same time. She was saluted with a hearty curse by one of the neighbors and told we had fired our house ourselves the second time on purpose! I ran about inquiring for my wife and other children; met the chief man and constable of the town going from my house, not toward it to help me. I took him by the hand and said 'God's will be done.' His answer was, 'Will you never have done with your tricks? You fired your house, once before; did you not get enough by it then that you have done it again?' This was cold comfort. I said 'God forgive you! I find you are chief man still.' I heard my wife was saved; I fell on mother earth and blessed God.

"I went to her. She was alive, and could just speak. She thought I had perished and so did all the rest nor any share of the children for a quarter of an hour. By this time all the chambers and everything was consumed to ashes, for the fire was stronger than a furnace, the violent wind beating it down on the house.

"She told me afterwards how she escaped. When I first opened the back door she endeavored to force through the fire at the foxdoor but was struck back twice to the ground. She thought to have died there, but prayed to Christ to help her. She found new strength, got up alone and waded through two or three yards of flame, the fire on the ground being up to her knees. She had nothing on but her shoes and a wrapping gown and one coat on her arm. This she wrapped about her breast and got through safe into the yard, but not a soul yet to help her. She never looked up or spoke till I came; only when they brought her last child to her bade them lay it on the bed. *This was the lad who I heard cry in the house, but God saved him almost by a miracle. He was forgot by the servants in a hurry. He ran to the window toward the yard, stood on a chair and cried for help. There were now a few people gathered, one of whom loves me helped up another to the window. The child, seeing a man come into the window was frightened and ran away to get to his mother's room. He could not open the door so he ran back again. The man was fallen down from the window, and all the bed and hangings in the room where he was were blazing. They helped up the man a second time and poor John leaped into his arms and was saved.* I could not believe it until I had kissed him two or three times. My wife then said to me 'Are your books safe?' I told her it was not much. Now she and all the rest were preserved. I hope my wife will recover and not miscarry but God will give me my nineteenth child. She has burnt her legs but they mend. When I came to her her lips were black. I did not know her. Some of the children are a little burnt, but not hurt or disfigured. I only got a small blister on my hand. The neighbors sent us clothes for it is cold without them."

The child "Kezzy" was born and lived. Wesley picked up a torn leaf of his Polyglot Bible on which these words alone were legible "Vade; vende omnia quot habes; et attolle crucem, et sequere me." He had come to Epworth poor; now, 15 years later, he was poorer, having doggedly served his parishioners only to have them detest him. "But, he stood unbeaten; and as he stared out his window there gripped him—not for the first time, a fierce ironical affection for the hard landscape, the fields of his striving, even the folk who had proved such good haters. . . . With him as with many; true men disappointed in his fate, his hopes passed from himself to fasten the more eagerly on his sons. He wanted them to be great and eminent soldiers of Christ, and he divined already that if for one above the others, this eminence was reserved for John" (All information taken from Quiller-Couch, *Hetty Wesley,* pp. 68ff).

JOHN WESLEY'S ENEMIES

We hear of the blessings of revival. But, what was it like to stand before the enemies of such a revival and preach? Again from Quiller-Couches' biography comes this moving account:

"All the world has heard how John Wesley rode into Epworth; and how, his father's pulpit having been denied to him, he stood outside on his father's tomb and preached evening after evening in the warm June weather the Gospel of justification by faith to the listening crowd.

"Eight evenings he preached from it, and on the third evening chose for his text: 'Unto him that worketh not, but believe on Him that justifieth the ungodly, his faith is counted to him for righteousness.'"

Under the sycamore, by the churchyard wall a little distance from the crowd, a man stood and listened—a clergyman with a worn black gown, a man not old in years but with a face prematurely old and shoulders already stooped under the burden of life—John Whitelamb. He watched lingering between fear and hope of being recognized. When the preacher mounted the slab, stroked his hair, and turned his face toward the sycamore, fixing his eyes (as it seemed) upon the figure, Whitelamb felt sure he had been recognized; a moment later he doubted whether that gaze had passed over him in forgetfulness or contempt. They had been too hard for him, these Wesleys. They had all departed from Epworth, years before, and had left him who had been their brother alone with his miserable doubts. No letters, no message of remembered affection or present good-will ever came from them. He had been unfaithful to his religion; they had cast him off. For seven years, he had walked and labored among the men and women here gathered in the midsummer dusk; but the faces to which he had turned for comfort were faces of the past—some dead, others far away.

So the preacher's voice came as one rending the tomb "Son of man, can these bones live?" The bones of Christ's warrior beneath the slab, laid to rest in utter weariness, were stirring, putting forth strength and a voice which pierced Whitelamb's marrow. He listened, letting the tears run. Only once did he withdraw his eyes and then for a moment they fell on John Romely also loitering on the outskirts of the crowd and plainly two minds about interfering. Romely was, at this time, Curate of Epworth, delegate of an absentee sporting rector, and had in truth set this ball rolling by denying John Wesley his pulpit. He had miscalculated Wesley's flock; this stubborn English breed so loyal in enmity, loving the memory of a foe who had proven himself a man. Whitelamb watched with a loose-lipped sneer; too weak to conquer his own curiosity, far too weak to assert his authority and attempt to clear the churchyard of that "enthusiasm" which he had denounced in his most florid style the past Sunday within the church.

"He heard men and women—notorious evil-livers, some of them crying aloud. Ah, the great simplicity of it was beyond him! And yet not perhaps beyond him, could he believe the truth in the bygone years never questioned by him that Jesus Christ was very God. He waited for the last word, and strode back to his lonely home with a mind unconvinced yet wondering at the power he had witnessed, a heart bursting with love.

"He sat down to write at once but tore up many letters. With Christ, to believe was to be forgiven. If Christ could not be tender to doubt, how much less would John Wesley be tender? It was not until he found courage to dispatch the following:

"Dear Brother:

"I saw you at Epworth on Tuesday evening. Fain would I have spoken to you, but that I am quite at a loss to know how to address or behave to you. Your way of thinking is so extraordinary that your presence creates an awe, as if you were an inhabitant of another world. God grant you and your followers may always have entire liberty of conscience. Will you not allow others the same?

"I noticed I cannot think as you do, any more than I can help honoring and loving you. Dear sir, will you credit me? I retain the highest veneration and affection for you. The sight of you moves me strangely. My heart overflows with gratitude. I feel in a higher degree all that tenderness and yearning with which I am affected toward every branch of the

Wesley family. I cannot refrain from tears when I reflect, is this the man who at Oxford was more than a father to me; is this he whom I have heard expound, or dispute publicly or preach with such applause—and oh that I should ever add—whom I have heard lately preach at Epworth on his father's tombstone? I am quite forgot. None of the family ever honor me with a line. Have I been ungrateful? I have been passionate, fickle, a fool; but I hope I shall never be ungrateful. Dear sir, is it in my power to serve or oblige you in any way? Glad I should be you would make use of me. God open all our eyes and lead us into truth wherever it be!"

The answer was delivered to him that same evening. It read:

"Dear Brother: I take you at your word if indeed it covers permission to preach in your church at Wroote on Sunday morning next. I design to take for text—and God grant it may be profitable to you and to others! —'Ask and it shall be given you.'"(All information taken from Quiller-Couch, *Hetty Wesley*.)

GEORGE WHITEFIELD
1714-1770

"Of all the spiritual heroes of a hundred years ago, none saw so soon as Whitefield what the times demanded and none were so forward in the great work of spiritual aggression" (Ryle, *Christian Leaders of the 18th Century,* p. 31).

Into the spiritual barrenness of the day came another friend of John Wesley who became quite the opposite of him in theology, mannerisms, and style. As a boy a self-confessed liar, thief and a gambler, addicted to filthy talk, cursing, foolishness and fantasy (like many of the boys his age), George Whitefield had a love for novels, plays, and a talent for mimicking ministers. His parents ran a hotel tavern called the "Bell Inn" where he lived for the first sixteen years of his life among highway robbers who picked their victims and planned attacks around the tables, and pimps who plied their trade among the customers. Here, he developed a vivid imagination, and a voice which became so powerful and expressive, that it was later apocryphally rumored that on a clear day you could hear him for five miles! (David Garrick, the top celebrated Shakespearian actor of his day said he would give "100 guineas to be able to say the word 'Oh!' like George Whitefield.")

Unlike Wesley, George did not grow up a church kid. From eight to fifteen, he lived in a home that was poor, with a stepfather and his mother who had been disillusioned, hurt, and finally surrendered to a broken marriage. Sent off on his own at 17 to Oxford for a chance to make it in life, he began to re-evaluate his ways and think about his future. Convicted and lonely, under the dealings of the Holy Spirit, he became deadly serious about spiritual things; and in 1733 Charles Wesley invited him to join the Oxford "Holy Club". This gathering for spiritual discipline, Bible study, and prayer, though an object of Deist and Rationalist scoffing on campus, was not evangelical, famous, or even significant to the revival to come. It was only a legal attempt, by the Wesleys and others, to be better people. But, it did not really meet any of their deep, inner needs. Here, young George read Henry Scougals' book *The Life of God in the Soul of a Man*, and it so directly contradicted all he believed that it alarmed him. In response to what he'd read, he said:

"God showed me I must be born again or be damned! I learned a man may go to church, say his prayers, receive the sacraments and yet not be a Christian . . . . Shall I burn this book? Shall I throw it down? Or shall I search it? I did search it; and holding the book in my hand thus addressed the God of heaven and earth: 'Lord, if I am not a Christian, or if I am not a real one, for Jesus Christ's sake show me what Christianity is that I may not be damned at last' . . . from that moment . . . did I know that I must become a new creature" (Whitefield, *Journals,* p. 52).

Then followed not faith but a fearfully increased

asceticism, with Whitefield wearing patched gown, dirty shoes, eating the worst food, "whole days and weeks...spent lying prostrate on the ground...bidding Satan depart from me in the name of Jesus ...begging for freedom from those proud hellish thoughts that used to crowd in upon and distract my soul" (Whitefield, *Journals,* p. 52).

For a year, the fearful pressure almost drove him mad, ruined his studies, and finally cost him his friendship in the Holy Club; he felt that perhaps his love for the other members was the final idolatry holding him back. Two years earlier, another Club member, William Morgan, had lost his mind and his life; now Whitefield, grimly resolved to "die or conquer" seemed about to do the same. Finally, at the end of all human resources, God revealed Himself to the overjoyed young zealot. A Gospel faith gave him the peace he had struggled so long to attain, and he wrote: "Oh what joy—joy unspeakable—joy full and big with glory was my soul filled when the weight of sin came off, and an abiding sense of the pardoning love of God and a full assurance of faith broke in on my...soul!"

Sunday, June 27, in the church of St. Mary de Crypt, he preached his first sermon. His mother, relatives, Robert Raikes, the founder of the Sunday-School, and some 300 other people crowded impatiently together to hear him. It was a startling introduction. Fifteen people were, said the presiding Bishop, "driven mad!" Whitefield was twenty-one years old. Thus began the "preaching that startled the nation." Ryle says, "From the very first he

obtained a degree of popularity such as no preacher
before or since has probably ever reached....No
preacher has ever been so universally popular in
every country he visited, in England, Scotland and
America. No preacher has ever retained his hold on
his hearers so entirely as he did for 34 years. His
popularity never waned. It was as great at the end of
his day as it was at the beginning...." (Ryle, *Christian Leaders Of The 18th Century,* p. 49). "Week-
days or Sundays, wherever he preached the churches
were crowded and an immense sensation produced.
The plain truth is that a really eloquent extempore
preacher preaching the pure Gospel with most
uncommon gifts of voice and manner was at that
time an entire novelty in London. Congregations
were taken by surprise and carried by storm."

He attracted high and low, rich and poor alike.
Eminent critics and literary men like Lord Bolingbroke and Lord Chesterfield were frequently his
delighted hearers. Bolingbroke said, "He is the most
extraordinary man in our times. He has the most
commanding eloquence I ever heard in any person.
Ben Franklin, the calculating Quaker by profession,
spoke in no measure terms of his preaching powers;
Hume the historian said it was worth riding twenty
miles to hear him" (Ryle, *Christian Leaders Of The
18th Century,* pp. 35-36).

None of the 75 recorded sermons under his name
do him justice; shorthand recorded without correc-
tion, they are terribly disjointed and dismembered.
He was exceptionally simple, lucid, bold, direct, and
full of the Gospel. "He met men face to face, like one

who had a message from God to them, 'I have come here to speak to you about your soul'" (Ryle, *Christian Leaders Of The 18th Century,* p. 52). He dramatized so vividly that sermons seemed to move and walk before your eyes, drawing such vivid pictures his hearers sometimes actually believed they saw and heard them. Lord Chesterfield was so entranced by Whitefield's description of the sinner as a blind beggar that when he moved him to the edge of a cliff, about to take the final fatal step he actually "made a rush forward to save him, exclaiming aloud 'He is gone! He is gone!'" (Dallimore, *George Whitefield,* Vol. II, p. 388). He was tremendously earnest; one poor uneducated man said, "He preached like a lion. His sermons were life and fire; you must listen whether you like to or not. There was a holy violence about him which firmly took your attention by storm." Of himself, Whitefield remarked, "I have not come in my own name. No! I have come in the Name of the Lord of hosts (and he brought down his hand and foot with a force that made the room ring) and I must and will be heard!" (Ryle, *Christian Leaders Of The 18th Century,* p. 54).

His sermons were filled with *immense feeling and pathos.* He commonly wept profusely in the pulpit; Cornelius Winter, who later often traveled with him, said he had not seen him get through a sermon without a tear. This was no affectation; he felt deeply for the souls before him. His sincerity awakened affections and touched secret springs which no amount of reasoning and demonstration could have moved. It smoothed down prejudices; they could not hate a man who wept so much over their souls. "I came to hear you with a pocket full of stones to break your head," said one convert, "but your sermon got the better of me, and God broke my heart." His *actions, voice, and fluency of language* were of the highest order; his manner in the pulpit was so curiously graceful and fascinating it was said that no one could hear him for five minutes without forgetting that he squinted.

Under Wesley's request, Whitefield went to Georgia for about a year to help with the Savannah Orphan House set up for children of the colonists. On his return, the bulk of the Anglican clergy were no longer favorable to him. Scandalized by preaching regeneration or the "new birth" as a thing which many baptized persons greatly needed, many began to denounce him openly, and deny him pulpits. Ryle says, "The plain truth is that the Church of England of that day was not ready for a man like Whitefield ....too much asleep to understand him and vexed at a man who would not keep still and leave the devil alone" (Ryle, *Christian Leaders Of The 18th Century,* p. 39). The door to the Church of England's ministry began to close, and Whitefield, seeing thousands out of church, resolved in a "spirit of holy aggression" to go out into the highways and byways and compel them to come in. His first attempt was among the Kingswood colliers near Bristol, in February of 1739. He began on a hill to speak to about one or two hundred of these coal miners on Matthew 5:1-3. He said of them:

"Having no righteousness of their own to

renounce, they were glad to hear of Jesus who was a friend to publicans and came not to call the righteous but sinners to repentance. The first discovery of their being affected was the sight of the white gutters made by their tears which fell plentifully down their black cheeks as they came out of the coal-pits....Sometimes when twenty thousand people were before me, I had not in my own apprehension a word to say either to God or them. But I was never totally deserted....The open heavens above me, the prospect of the adjacent fields with the sight of thousands, some in coaches, some on horseback, and some in the trees and at all times affected and in tears was almost too much for me, and quite overcame me" (Whitefield, *Journals,* p. 223).

The word spread; the next audience was 2,000; the third 4,000 to 5,000, and then audiences multiplied and expanded, 10,000, 14,000, 20,000! Shortly, he would be preaching to up to 30,000 people at one time. Thousands came to hear him preach at 6:00 a.m. in the snow; whole cities turned out to hear the young man with the golden voice and a supernatural authority from heaven. From 1739 until his death in 1770, 31 years of immense effect, his life was one uniform outreach, his vision one thing: preach Christ, and entreat men to repent and be saved. In a Deist nation, God often supernaturally moved to confirm His reality and power in his meetings. In Yorkshire, with Lady Huntingdon, about to preach from a gallows scaffold on the text "It is appointed unto man once to die," a wild, terrifying shriek came from the audience; Grimshaw, one of his workers pressed through the crowd and cried, "Brother Whitefield; you stand amongst the dead and the dying; an immortal soul has been called into eternity, the destroying angel is passing over the congregation. Cry aloud and spare not!" (*Biographical Sketches Of Eminent Christians,* "George Whitefield," pp. 20-21). After a momentary silence, he began again, only to hear a second shriek and a second man fall dead near where Lady Huntingdon and Lady Margaret Ingham were standing. After that, the entire mass of the people seemed, predictably enough, "overwhelmed" by his appeal. God had found another man He could trust; Whitefield was a light-sabre in His hand for the nations. In one single week after preaching at Moorfields, he received one thousand letters from people under spiritual concern, and admitted 350 people to communion.

He worked tirelessly, like his friend Wesley, embarrassing in his zeal. He usually rose at 4:00 a.m. and spent whole nights in reading and devotions, sometimes getting up after going to bed at his usual hour of 10:00 p.m. to do so. He preached morning, afternoon, and evening on Sundays; 6:00 every morning and evening Monday to Thursday, and Saturday night; twelve messages a week, sometimes *forty to sixty* hours of speaking each week. At the same time, he carried on massive correspondence with people in almost every part of the world. In the thirty-four years of his ministry, he visited almost every town in England, Scotland, and Wales, crossed the Atlantic seven times, capturing souls in Boston, New York, and Philadelphia, and publicly preached an estimated 18,000 messages. Yet, this was no grim-lipped determination like his Oxford days. He was so singularly happy that one New York woman, speaking of the influences of the Holy Spirit that had won her, said, "Mr Whitefield was so cheerful it tempted me to become a Christian." He had a deep humility, and broad charity toward others, loving all others who loved Jesus in sincerity. If other Christians misrepresented him, he forgave them; if they refused to work with him, he still loved them. Whitefield, influenced deeply by Jonathan Edwards, was a Calvinist; Wesley, the scholar, moved toward a more Armenian view of the Gospel. One censorious professor of religion, knowing the sharp theological differences between them, asked if Whitefield thought he would see John Wesley in heaven. "I fear not," he said, "he will be so near the throne and we at such a distance that we shall hardly get a sight of him."

Most of his adult life George Whitefield was as "famous as any man in the English-speaking world. From the age of 22 till his death he was the foremost figure of the immense religious movement holding the multitudes' attention both sides of the Atlantic" (Ryle, *Christian Leaders Of The 18th Century,* p. 31).

Arnold Dallimore said in the preface to his massive and definitive two-volume study of Whitefield:

"This book was written with the desire—perhaps in a measure of inner certainty—that we shall see the great Head of the Church once more bring into being His special instruments of revival, that He will again raise up unto Himself certain young men whom He may use in this glorious employ. And what manner of men will they be? Men mighty in the Scriptures, their lives dominated by a sense of the greatness, the majesty and holiness of God, and their minds and hearts aglow with the great truths of the doctrines of grace. They will be men who have learned what it is to die to self, to human aims and personal ambitions; men who are willing to be 'fools for Christ's sake' who will bear reproach and false-hood, who will labor and suffer and whose desire will be, not to gain earth's accolades, but to win the Master's approbation when they appear before His awesome judgment seat. They will be men who will preach with broken hearts and tear-filled eyes, and upon whose ministries God will grant an extraordi-nary effusion of the Holy Spirit and who will witness 'signs and wonders following' in the transformation of multitudes of human lives. Indeed this book goes forth with the earnest prayer that amidst the ram-pant iniquity and glaring apostasy of the twentieth century, God will use it toward the raising up of such men and toward the granting of a mighty revival such as was witnessed two hundred years ago" (Dal-limore, *George Whitefield,* p. 16).

Whitefield died as suddenly as he had lived, almost literally "in harness" during one of his U.S. tours at Newbury Port, Sunday, September 29th, 1770 of a single spasmodic fit of asthma (almost before his friends knew he was ill), at the compara-tively early age of 56. Though ill and tired, he preached his last open-air sermon the day before on

2 Corinthians 13:5 to a huge crowd. He prayed, "Lord Jesus, I am weary in Thy work but not of Thy work. If I have not yet finished my course let me go and speak for Thee once more in the fields, seal Thy truth and come home and die" (J.R. Andrews, *Life Of George Whitefield,* p. 385). He ate with a friend, rode on to Newbury Port though terribly tired, and went to turn in early. Tradition says as he was headed for bed with a lighted candle in his hand he could not resist the opportunity to turn at the head of the stairs to speak to friends who had come to meet him; the candle burned downed to the socket before he quit! "Sudden death," he had often said, "is sudden glory. Whether right or not I cannot help wishing I may go off in the same manner. To me it would be worse than death to live to be nursed and to see friends weeping about me" (Ryle, *Christian Leaders Of The 18th Century,* p. 42).

From Whitefield, we learn this: God can use anyone who loves enough to care, and gives without sparing a gift of utter devotion to Him.

JONATHAN EDWARDS
1703-1764

At the same time God had raised up Whitefield
and Wesley, He was doing something unusual in the
United States among the young people of Northampton, Massachusetts. His instrument was Jonathan Edwards, recognized today as one of the most
original and creative native U.S. minds of all time,
later a President of Princeton. Here was a man who
often studied thirteen hours a day, whose writing
and eyesight were so bad he had to screw his face
down close to a sermon manuscript to read it (in a
monotone) and who inherited his Grandfather's
church so dead he described it succinctly as "Dry
Bones." Edwards was a convinced Calvinist, though
his modified view of sin as selfishness and virtue
defined as "disinterested benevolence" or "love to
intelligent being in proportion to the amount of
being each possesses" (Richard Lovelace, *Dynamics
Of Spiritual Life,* p. 364) gave him a commendable
evangelical and social concern. As a young man
believing that Christ died for all, and not the elect
only, he preached Christ's death as a sacrifice to
"general justice," a governmental theory of the cross
that both dominated New England thinking until
after the middle of the nineteenth century and produced a great missionary impulse. His most famous
(and much maligned) sermon, *Sinners In The Hands*

Of An Angry God, in which he said things like "The God Who dreadfully abhors you. . . Who dangles you over the precipice much as one would dangle a spider over a flame" was not at all typical of his preaching. Edwards' astonishing results on the day he preached that sermon are probably much more due to the manifested power of God in answer to prayer than some convicting content in his message.

Nevertheless, the effect was awesome; people screamed aloud, clutched the backs of pews and the stone pillars of the church, lest the ground open and swallow them alive into hell! The congregations of his day were full of lost people who attended for the social or political influence membership conferred; the pulpits likewise. "It seemed," he wrote, "to be a time of extraordinary dullness in religion; licentiousness prevailed among the youth of the town" (Edwards, *Thoughts On The Revival In New England*). These church kids ignored their parents (who were into land and affluence), walked the streets, and partied all night. They hit the bars and lived lewdly; if they lived in our day they would no doubt have been "users, cruisers, and boozers." Yet, as Harold A. Fischer notes, "Edwards' town was mild as far as being an example of. . . the prevalent sins of New England. . . the state of society and morals were becoming more and more corrupt. For a time it appeared as if God had forsaken New England" (Fischer, *Reviving Revivals,* pp. 152-153).

When two young people died unexpectedly, some of Edwards' sermons began to get through to people. By December 1734, half-a-dozen of the congregation got saved; after one girl, "who had been a bold flirt," was converted, others became concerned. God was on the loose in New England; the young rebels of the town began to turn to Christ, and, as Lovelace puts it, it became the "Jesus Movement" of its generation as the "hearts of the fathers were turned to their children and the children to their fathers" (Lovelace, *Dynamics Of Spiritual Life,* p. 38). A "great and earnest concern" about eternity and spiritual things gripped all social classes and ages. It accelerated rapidly until souls came as it were "by flocks to Jesus;" about three hundred in six months. In the "spring and summer following 1735," noted Edwards, "the town seemed to be full of the presence of God as it never was so full of love, nor so full of joy, and yet so full of distress as it was then. . . . Our public assemblies were then beautiful; the congregation was alive in God's service, every one earnestly intent on the public worship, every hearer eager to drink in the words of the minister. . . the assembly . . . from time to time in tears while the Word was preached; some weeping with joy and distress, others with joy and love—still others in pity and concern for the souls of their neighbors" (Fischer, *Reviving Revivals,* p. 158).

It was the beginning of the "most far-reaching and transformed event of the eighteenth-century religious life of America"—the revival that became known as *The Great Awakening.* The analogue of German Pietism and British Methodism, it "emphasized conversion as the normal entrance into the Kingdom of God; gave general diffusion to the

Congregational view of the church as a company of experiential Christians" (Walker, *History Of The Christian Church,* p. 571).

The wave kept spreading through other communities and towns; Connecticut, New York, New Jersey; ultimately affecting over a hundred towns. Edwards' record and analysis of the revival, "A Narrative of Surprising Conversion," crossed the Atlantic to Welsey, who wrote, "Surely this is the Lord's doing and it is marvellous in our eyes." It prepared the way for the young spiritual ignitionist, George Whitefield, who would travel across the nation, "digging trenches" between the filling pools of spiritual power.

On Whitefield's second visit to Philadelphia, Benjamin Franklin said, "The multitudes of all sects and denominations that attended his sermons were enormous...it was wonderful to see the change so soon made in the manners of the inhabitants. From being thoughtless and indifferent about religion, it seemed as if all the world was growing religious; one could not walk through a town in an evening without hearing psalms sung in different families in every street" (Fischer, *Reviving Revivals,* p. 155).

Joining Edwards were men like Gilbert Tennant. Though "less polished" than Edwards, his sermons had such power that Reverend Jonathan Parsons reported of his ministry in Lyme, Connecticut, "Many had their countenances changed; their thoughts seemed to trouble them, so that their loins were loosed and their knees smote one against the other. Great numbers cried aloud in the anguish of their souls. Several stout men fell as though a cannon had been discharged and a ball made its way through their hearts. Some young women were greatly disturbed" (Fischer, *Reviving Revivals,* p. 156). Under Tennant, and other preachers like Blair, Finley, Dickenson, and Davies, the work spread through the Middle Colonies, and by 1743, the South. Through the prayer and missionary effort of Edwards' son-in-law, David Brainerd, it even reached the Indians. In twenty years, between 25,000 and 50,000 were added to the churches—over a hundred percent increase in both churches and preachers during this massive revival. Thus, it justly deserves the title "The First Great Awakening."

EDWARDS ON REVIVAL

Jonathan Edwards wrote in great detail describing, and later defending, this *First Great Awakening*. What did he think of the nature of a true work of God? In his account of the work, he writes:

"The highest transports I have been acquainted with, the affections of admiration, love and joy, so far as another could judge, have been raised to the highest pitch, and the following things have been united:

"A very frequent dwelling for some considerable time together in view of the glories of the Divine perfections and Christ's excellencies...the soul has been as it were perfectly overwhelmed and swallowed up with light and love, a sweet solace, and a rest and a joy of soul altogether unspeakable. The person has more than once continued for five or six hours together without interruption in a clear and lively sense of the infinite beauty and amiableness of Christ's Person and the heavenly sweetness of His transcendent love.... The heart was swallowed up in a kind of glow of Christ's love coming down as a constant stream of sweet light, at the same time the soul all flowing out in love to Him; so that there seemed to be a constant flowing and reflowing from heart to heart. The soul dwelt on high, was lost in God and seemed almost to lose the body....Extraordinary views of Divine things and the religious affections were frequently attended with very great effects on the body. . . . The person was deprived of all ability to speak. Sometimes the hands were clenched and the flesh cold but the senses remaining. Animal nature was often in a great emotion and agitation and the soul so overcome with admiration and a kind of omnipotent joy as to cause the person unavoidably to leap with all his might in joy and mighty exaltation.

"Nearly three years ago they greatly increased upon an extraordinary self-dedication, renunciation of the world and resignation of all to God, which were made in a great view of God's excellency in high exercise of love to Him and rest and joy in Him. . . . All that is pleasant and glorious and all that is terrible in this world seemed perfectly to vanish into nothing and nothing to be left but God, in whom the soul was perfectly swallowed up as in an infinite ocean of blessedness.

"This great rejoicing has been with trembling, i.e. attended with a deep and lively sense of the greatness and majesty of God and the person's own exceeding littleness and vileness. Spiritual joys. . .were never attended with the least appearance of laughter or lightness either of the countenance or the manner of speaking; but with a peculiar abhorrence of such appearances in spiritual rejoicing. These high transports, when past have had abiding effects in the increase of sweetness, rest and humility which they have left upon the soul; and a new engagedness of heart to live to God's honor and watch and fight against sin" (Edwards, *Works Of Jonathan Edwards,* p. 301).

A charge critics often made when the work of revival seriously began to threaten established values and traditions was, "enthusiasm," or what we would call fanatacism. Edwards, in common with others in the First Great Awakening, gave little importance to any spiritual gifts or manifestations which smacked of fleshy demonstrations. He makes two important comments felt when the spirit of a true revival is manifest:

"These transporting views and rapturous affections are not attended with any enthusiastic dispositions to follow impulses, or any supposed prophetical revelations; nor have they been observed to be attended with any appearance of spiritual pride but very much of a contrary disposition—an increase of humility and meekness and a disposition in honor to prefer others ....These two things were felt in a remarkable manner: (1) A peculiar AVERSION TO JUDGING other professing Christians of good standing in the visible church with respect to their conversion or degrees of grace; or at all intermeddling with that matter so much as to determine against and condemn others in the thoughts of the heart. Such want of candor appeared hateful, as not agreeing with that lamb-like humility, meekness, gentleness and charity which the soul then above other times saw to be beautiful. (2) Secondly...was a very great sense of the importance of MORAL SOCIAL DUTIES and how great a part of religion lay in them. There was such a new sense and conviction of this beyond what had been before that it seemed to be as it were a clear discovery was made to the soul."

Edwards noted the following characteristics of revival:

(a) "An extraordinary sense of the aweful (*sic*) majesty, greatness and HOLINESS OF GOD so as sometimes to overwhelm soul and body; a sense of the piercing, all-seeing eye of God so as to sometimes take away the bodily strength; and an extraordianry view of the infinite terribleness of the WRATH OF GOD, together with a sense of the ineffable misery of sinners exposed to this wrath.

(b) "Especially longing after these two things; viz to be MORE PERFECT in HUMILITY and ADORATION. The flesh and the heart seem often to cry out, lying low before God and adoring Him with greater love and humility. . . . The person felt a great delight in singing praises to God and Jesus Christ, and longing that this present life may be as it were one continued song of praise to God. There was a longing as one person expressed it, 'to sit and sing this life away'; and an overcoming pleasure in the thoughts of spending an eternity in that exercise. Together with living by faith to a great degree, there was a constant and extraordinary distrust of our own strength and wisdom; a great dependence on God for His help in order to the performance of any thing to God's acceptance and being restrained from the most horrid sins."

Thus, the convicting Spirit of God was the impetus to lead on to further revival and deeper awakening. The new American frontiers were crying for repentence and revival, and their needs were met in the "Second Great Awakening."

PART III

The Second Great Awakening

1800's

THE SECOND GREAT AWAKENING

Doctrinal division and party politics had hurt the results of the First Great Awakening. A flood of Rationalistic literature came from France and Great Britain which Dr. Timothy Dwight described as "the dregs of infidelty vomited on us...the whole mass of pollution emptied on this country. An enormous edition of the *Age of Reason,* by Thomas Paine, was published in France and sold in America for a few cents; and where it could not be sold, it was given away" (Fischer, *Reviving Revivals,* p. 162). The effect on U.S. colleges was disastrous; students looking for an excuse to rebel against the society of the day embraced rationalism and called themselves by the names of famous skeptics and infidels. Bible Colleges became centers of skepticism; Christian students became such a minority that on some campuses they felt compelled to meet secretly. In shades of the radical movements of the late 1960's, students of those days held mock communion services, forced the resignation of a Bible College President, and attempted to blow up a campus building. But, God had a surprise in store; college preachers began to see conviction spreading as they counter-attacked by powerful sermons filled with relentless logic and often very real anointing. And even along the early frontier in Daniel Boone's day, some powerful revivals broke out. In his book, *The Awakening That Must Come,* Lewis A. Drummond, Billy Graham Chair of Evangelism professor at Southern Baptist Theological Seminary, describes these powerful frontier revivals in the days of Daniel Boone. This movement, in the late 1780's was thus part of the Second Great Awakening:

"Caught up in the awakening were two North Carolina Presbyterian ministers, James McGready and his protege, Barton Stone.... Trekking through the Cumberland Gap they took up their ministries in Kentucky" (Drummond, *The Awakening That Must Come,* p. 14).

McGready was an "impassioned preacher, diligent pastor, and fervent man of prayer." In June of 1800, he called on the people of south-central Kentucky to gather for a four-day extended observance of the Lord's Supper. People came expecting blessing, and God met their faith; the Holy Spirit fell on them powerfully. Barton Stone, later a leader of the Disciples of Christ, said, "There on the edge of the prairie...multitudes came together.... The scene was new and passing strange. It baffled description. Many, very many fell down as men slain in battle, and continued for hours together in an apparently breathless and motionless state, sometimes for a few moments reviving and exhibiting symptoms of life by a deep groan or piercing shriek, or a prayer for mercy fervently uttered" (Fischer, *Reviving Revivals,* p. 165-166). Friday and Saturday saw floods of repentant tears, and then times of exuberant rejoicing. The climax came on the final day when John

McGee, a Methodist minister, gave the closing exhortation. His own words:

"I...exhorted them to let the Lord omnipotent reign in their hearts and submit to Him and their souls should live.... I turned again and losing sight of the fear of man, I went through the house shouting and exhorting with all possible ecstasy and energy and the floor was soon covered by the slain" (Drummond, *The Awakening That Must Come,* p. 15).

People had come in unprecedented numbers from the hundred-mile radius of the Red River. Because there was insufficient housing, they brought bedrolls and tents for temporary housing; thus, the first camp meeting was born.

"No person seemed to wish to go home," said McGready, "hunger and sleep seemed to affect nobody—eternal things were the vast concerns.... Sober professors who had been communicants for many years now were lying prostrate on the ground crying out in such language as this 'Oh! How I would have despised any person a few days ago who would have acted as I am doing now! But I cannot help it!'...persons of every description, white and black, were to be found in every part of the multitude crying out for mercy in the most extreme distress" (Drummond, *The Awakening That Must Come,* pp. 15-16).

THE CANE RIDGE REVIVAL

Barton Stone, at the invitation of Daniel Boone, preached and served at the Cane Ridge Meeting House in Bourbon County. Stone was so overwhelmed by the Red River revival that he went home and, in May, 1801, called for a similar meeting in Cane Ridge, "which was attended with blessing." A second meeting in August was then called; to the utter astonishment of all, over 20,000 people arrived for the six-day camp meeting! It was an incredible event, for this was the sparsely populated frontier. Among the thousands converted was James B. Finley, who later became a Methodist circuit rider. He wrote:

"The noise was like the roar of Niagra. The vast sea of human beings seemed to be agitated as if by a storm. I counted seven ministers, all preaching at one time, some on stumps, others in wagons and one standing on a tree which had, in falling, lodged against another.... Some of the people were singing, others praying, some crying for mercy in the most piteous accents, while others were shouting most vociferously. While witnessing these scenes, a peculiarly-strange sensation such as I had never felt before came over me. My heart beat tumultuously, my knees trembled, my lips quivered and I felt as though I must fall to the ground. A strange super-

114

natural power seemed to pervade the entire mass of mind there collected.... I stepped up on a log where I could have a better view of the surging sea of humanity. The scene that then presented itself to my mind was indescribable. At one time I saw at least five hundred swept down in a moment as if a battery of a thousand guns had been opened upon them and then immediately followed shrieks and shouts that rent the very heavens" (Mendell Taylor, *Exploring Evangelism,* p. 142).

The American frontier was set ablaze. The Presbyterians and Methodists immediately caught fire, and then the flame broke out among the Baptists in Carroll County on the Ohio River. Great personalities emerged from this awakening. Men like Peter Cartwright, Charles Finney, and the Methodist circuit riders. Baptist revivalism had its birth in this movement; the camp meeting motif spread all over eastern America. The frontier was radically transformed. Instead of gambling, cursing, and vice, spirituality and genuine Christianity characterized the early westward movement. It was God's great hour. Revival stopped skepticism in its tracks and returned the helm of the country to the godly.

CHARLES FINNEY
1792-1875

"When he opened his mouth he was aiming a gun. When he spoke bombardment began. The effects of his speaking were almost unparalleled in modern history. Over half a million people were converted through his ministry... in an age when there were no amplifiers or mass communications, he spearheaded a revival which literally altered the course of history" (Miller, *Charles Finney,* cover).

Charles Finney was born the year after Wesley died; appropriately, because the revival events of Finney's life became the link from the First Great Awakening of one century to the Second Great Awakening of the next. Harvard professor Perry Miller wrote: "Charles Grandison Finney led America out of the eighteenth century" (Finney, *The Heart Of Truth,* cover). A tall (6'2"), impressive, blue-eyed young frontiersman from a totally non-Christian farming family, he was a musical, gently mocking pagan. Most available pictures and sketches (taken near the end of his life) do not do him justice. They do not capture his irrepressible sense of humor, his zest for life, or his rugged and athletic build. He was apparently deeply attractive and personable; why else would his first fiance have waited, sometimes for months when revivals broke out, for him to pick her up for the wedding? Their

116

deeply moving love is recorded in his private letters. Following her death, Finney was able to marry again, and two more times! An expert marksman, sailor, and athlete, "when he was twenty he excelled every man and boy he met in every species of toil or sport. No man could throw him, no man could knock his hat off, no man could run faster, jump further, leap higher or throw a ball with greater force and precision" (Edmon, *Finney Lives On,* pp. 25-26).

Though he regularly attended the gentle Dr. George Gales' Presbyterian church, he scorned prayer meetings because he "never saw any of their prayers answered." Nevertheless, he played bass viol, sang in the choir, and was in love with Lydia, one of the pretty, young Christian girls who attended there (later his first and deeply loved wife). Charles was then studying to be a lawyer. While reading *Blackstone's Law Commentaries,* then the ultimate authority on the subject, he was struck by this Christian's constant reference to the Bible as the basis for all civil and moral law. He obtained a copy and began to study it seriously. Perhaps of all the great evangelists and revivalists, Finney's originality and distinction owes much to the fresh approach he took, confronted for the first time by the truth of Scripture which he believed to be God's Word. He later noted:

"I often said to myself 'If these things are really taught in the Bible, I must be an infidel.' But the more I read my Bible the more clearly I saw that these things were not found there upon any fair principles of interpretation such as would be admitted in a court of justice.... But the Spirit of God conducted me through the darkness and delivered me from the labyrinth and fog of a false philosophy, and set my feet upon the rock of truth—as I trust" (Finney, from the Preface, *Systematic Theology,* p. x).

His conversion read like something from the book of Acts. Under deep conviction from the Scripture, and dealt with by the Holy Spirit, he vowed one October Sunday evening in the Fall of 1821, to "settle the question of my soul's salvation at once, that if it were possible I would make my peace with God" (Finney, *Autobiography,* p. 12).

For the next two days, his conviction increased, but he could not pray or weep; he felt if he could be alone and cry out aloud to God something might happen. Tuesday evening, he became so nervous he felt if he did cry out he would sink into hell, but survived until morning. Setting out for work, he was suddenly confronted by an "inward voice" that riveted him to the spot in front of his office. "What are you waiting for? Did you not promise to give your heart to God? What are you trying to do—work out a righteousness of your own?" The whole essence of conversion opened to him there in what he called "a marvelous manner"; the finished work of Christ, the need to give up his sins and submit to His righteousness. The voice continued, "Will you accept it, now, today?" Finney vowed "Yes; I will accept it today or I will die in the attempt" (Finney, *Autobiography,* p. 15).

Sneaking away over the hill to a small forest where he liked to take walks, avoiding anyone who might ask him what he was doing, the young lawyer fought a battle with his pride. Several times he tried to pray, but rustling leaves stopped him cold; he thought someone was coming and would see him trying to talk to God. Finally near despair, thinking he had rashly vowed and that his hard-heartedness had grieved away the Holy Spirit, he had a sudden revelation of his pride: "An overwhelming sense of my wickedness in being ashamed to have a human being see me on my knees before God took such powerful possession of me that I cried at the top of my voice... I would not leave that place if all men on earth and all the devils in hell surrounded me.... The sin appeared aweful (*sic*), infinite. It broke me down before the Lord" (Finney, *Autobiography,* p. 17).

Just then, a Scripture verse seemed to "drop into his mind with a flood of light": "Then shall you go and pray to Me and I will hearken to you. Then shall you seek Me and find Me when you search for Me with all your heart" (Jeremiah 29:13). It came to Finney with the flood of revelation, though he did not recall ever having read it. It shifted faith for him from the intellect to the choice; he knew that a God who could not lie had spoken to him and that his vow would be heard. Quietly, walking back toward the village, he was filled with such a sense of peace that it "seemed all nature listened." He realized it was noon; many hours had passed without any conscious sense of the passage of time.

Back at his office, his boss, Judge Wright, gone to

119

lunch, Finney took down his bass viol and began to play and sing some hymns. "But as soon as I began to sing these sacred words, I began to weep. It seemed as if my heart were all liquid; my feelings were in such a state that I could not hear my own voice in singing without causing my sensibility to overflow...I tried to suppress my tears, but could not" (Finney, *Autobiography,* p. 20).

All that afternoon, filled with a profound sense of tenderness, sweetness, and peace, he helped Judge Wright relocate their office. The work finished, he bade his employer goodnight. "I had accompanied him to the door; and as I closed the door and turned around my heart seemed to be liquid within me. All my feelings seemed to rise and flow out and the utterance of my heart was: 'I want to pour out my soul to God'" (Finney, *Autobiography,* p. 21). He rushed into a back room of the office to pray and then it happened:

"There was no fire, no light in the room; nevertheless it appeared to me as if it were perfectly light. As I went in and shut the door after me, it seemed as if I met the Lord Jesus Christ face to face. It did not occur to me then, nor did it for some time afterward, that it was a wholly mental state. On the contrary, it seemed to me that I saw Him as I would see any other man. He said nothing, but looked at me in such a manner as to break me down right at His feet...it seemed to me a reality that He stood before me and I fell down at His feet and poured out my soul to Him. I wept aloud like a child, and made such confessions as I could with a choked utterance. It seemed to me that I bathed His feet with my tears, and yet I had no distinct impression that I touched Him" (Finney, *Autobiography,* p. 21).

For a long time, Finney continued in this state; eventually he broke off the interview, and returned to the front office where the fire in the fireplace had nearly burned out. As he was about to take a seat by the fire, he received, in his own words, "a mighty baptism of the Holy Ghost. Without any expectation of it, without ever having the thought in my mind that there was any such thing for me, without any recollection that I had ever heard the thing mentioned by any person in the world, the Holy Spirit descended on me in a manner that seemed to go through me, body and soul. I could feel the impression, like a wave of electricity, going through and through me. Indeed, I could not express it any other way. It seemed like the very breath of God. I can recall distinctly that it seemed to fan me like immense wings.

"No words can express the wonderful love that was shed abroad in my heart. I wept aloud with joy and love; and I do not know but I should say, I literally bellowed out the unutterable gushings of my heart. These waves came over me and over me and over me, one after the other until I recollect I cried out 'I shall die if these waves continue to pass over me.' I said, 'Lord I cannot bear it any more.' Yet I had no fear of death" (Finney, *Autobiography,* p. 22).

Later, a church choir member, knocking on his door, found him loudly weeping and asked if he was sick or in pain. Eventually able to speak, Finney said, "No, but so happy that I cannot live." The following morning, with the sunlight, his baptism of power and love returned, and with it a call to the ministry. All that day each encounter with the lost led to powerful conviction and conversion. The first man he spoke to, (his boss, the Judge) was struck with such conviction of sin that he could not look at him. He left the office under deep conviction, and a few days later was converted in the same woods where Finney himself was saved. The second visitor, a client and a church deacon with a 10:00 a.m. case for the newly converted barrister to try for him, did not escape either. The young lawyer met him with the words, "I have a retainer from the Lord Jesus Christ to plead His cause and I cannot plead yours" (Finney, *Autobiography,* p. 26). The next, a Universalist in a Christian shoemaker's shop had his arguments demolished, and headed over the fence to the woods and salvation. From that day on, Finney realized it was goodbye to his legal profession. He launched out on a life of fire and power such as there have been few parallels in Christian history.

Like all other men of God, he had his faults. Sometimes extravagant and emotional in language, he was so careful to bring glory to God that he attacked anything that seemed in any way to him to harbor an attitude of resistance to God's Spirit. Later, analyzing the strengths and weaknesses of his own earlier ministry, he felt he had been too apt to teach and inform before bringing people up to their known obligation to submit to Christ; this he found did not encourage faith, but could lead to a cynical, fault-finding, rationalistic spirit in converts.

In later years, he put more emphasis on the power of the Holy Spirit and the simplicity of trust in Christ as the key to all victory and perseverance in ministry. Some estimate that over 80% of his converts during the revivals stayed true to Christ without ever backsliding, an awesome testimony to the power of a pure life and an urgent message of holiness. Despite his weakness, he nevertheless impacted cities with the subtlety of a hydrogen bomb. He refused to bow to prevailing Calvinist doctrines of no truly free human choices, "inherited sin," and born-damned children. He strongly stressed both the possibility and practicality of a Christian and Gospel perfection. His radical new measures of allowing women to pray, publicly naming those present in meetings resisting God, and extended meetings did not earn him any great favor with many fellow-ministers. Yet, it was impossible to ignore what he did and the vital impact his ministry had on the nation. Even his enemies and detractors admitted the awesome way God used him, although attributing it perhaps to his prayer life, the sovereignty of God, or the mood of the times, while avoiding the obvious implications of a theology and experience that was to break the back of a religious fatalism which had dominated the land.

Three things stand out in Finney's astonishing life: his willingness to change, his deep and loving devotional life and prayer, and his radical message of practical and immediate holiness. "Denounced by clergy and secularist alike for his innovations in evangelism, he was intolerably ahead of his time. One preacher (Lyman Beecher) threatened to oppose him with cannon if he dared venture into his parish" (Finney, *The Heart Of Truth,* cover). (Beecher later relented and extended an invitation to Finney.)

Finney's preaching stirred such emotion that his enemies counterattacked. "Swinging above your heads are two distorted figures suspended on ropes. At the touch of the torch they leap into flames and the crowd screams in sheer delight. Sound like a scene from a lynching... a race riot! Not at all. It is a religious gathering. The charred creatures smoldering in the air represent the public's expression of opposition to the preaching and praying of America's greatest evangelistic team. Charles Grandison Finney and his partner-in-prayer, Father Nash, have just been burned in effigy. Preachers and pew-warmers alike joined forces against the two men who did more to spearhead revival than any other pair in American history.... Finney became so incredibly alive that everywhere he went life leaped from him to others like flames in a fire-storm. It is impossible to read about this man without being shaken..." (Basil Miller, *Charles Finney-A Biography,* cover).

Some of the social implications of his message are dealt with in other sections of this book. It would be true to say that his life and writings influenced more people toward revival and social reform than any other preacher of the last century. "Most of Finney's life was lived before the Civil War. He hated slavery with a passion. He insisted it was impossible to be on the right side of God and the wrong side of the slavery issue at the same time. When he took the presidency of Oberlin College, he did so on the express condition that the institution be thoroughly integrated. His convictions were born in the fires of revival and shaped by a keen lawyer's mind committed to the full authority of the Bible. So effective were his theological writings that they have been the impetus for revivals around the world since his death" (Finney, *The Heart Of Truth*, cover).

Charles Finney was unquestionably the most impressive religious revolutionary that America has ever produced. When he first gave a public account of his own conversion, the tumult began. A fellow-lawyer left that meeting with the comment, "he is in earnest...but he is deranged" (Finney, *Finney On Revival*, cover). "When he stood up to preach his first revival messages in the backwoods regions of New York, startling chaos ensued. One man came to the meeting with a pistol, intent on killing the speaker of the evening. Instead he fell to the floor and was soundly saved. Everywhere he went for some forty years the tumult spread. Thousands found peace in believing. Fortunately, for the generations which have followed, Finney committed the secrets of dynamic evangelism to print...a handy introduction to Christian workers who would learn the simple principles which govern the promises of revival" (Finney, *Finney On Revival*, cover).

Many of his materials go into reprint generation after generation, being the source of desires for holy awakening. There is his biography, a deeply moving account of his ministry; *Reflections on Revivals,* a succinct analysis of his early mistakes and dangers; *Lectures To Professing Christians* and *Sermons On Gospel Themes* (re-arranged and re-issued under various titles), powerful attacks on compromise and counterfeit conversion. More recently, excerpts from the Oberlin Evangelist, a "Jesus Paper" he edited (issued during the revivals), have been issued under the titles "The Promise Of The Spirit" and "Principles Of Victory."

V. Raymond Edman, past president of Wheaton, said, "In all my reading on revival I have found nothing to be the equal of Finney's *Lectures on Revival.* They constitute lessons that God's servant learned in days when tens of thousands came to a saving knowledge of the Lord Jesus. I have found nothing more heart-searching, more pungent and powerful, and more satisfying than these messages by Finney" (Edman, from the Preface, *Finney Lives On*).

Of the perennial *Revival Lectures* it is said: "No other book on the subject has been so mightily used of God. It has been translated into many languages and circulated around the world. . . . In *Revival Lectures,* Finney explains what a revival of religion is and treats at length such related subjects as the place of faith and prayer in relation to revival; the need of the Holy Spirit; methods to be used in the quest for souls; hindrances to revivals; instructions to converts and helpful rules for growth in grace. The principles and methods God used so mightily in

Finney's day are equally effective in our own time"
(From the publisher's preface, *Lectures on Revivals
Of Religion*).

Finney's life spanned two mighty periods of
American and British Christian history, the First
and Second Great Awakenings. Outliving three
wives, radical to the last, he passed away peacefully
in Oberlin, on Sunday, August 16th, 1875. Written
on his tombstone are his memorable words, "The
Lord be with us as He was with our fathers; let us not
fail nor forsake Him."

CONTRIBUTIONS OF THE AWAKENINGS

Two awesome centuries of manifested power: the First and Second Great Awakenings, and up to the 1857 revival, were all escalating demonstrations of the greatness and glory of God at work in His people. While building on the strengths of the Reformation, the revivalists who followed corrected some of its weaknesses. They held Reform convictions of the absolute authenticity and inspiration of Scripture. They did not forget the great truths of justification by faith, the Lordship of Christ, and the sovereignty of God. They had also learned from their Puritan spiritual forefathers the call to discipline and holiness in the true child of God. But, no generation can master all God has in His heart for His Church. These next-generation believers went a step further than the Reformers were able to go. They restored or amplified some neglected facets of the Gospel we sorely need again today.

(1) *The Obligation of Man: Responsibility.*

It cannot be denied that early Reform zeal to stress God's ultimate Lordship and absolute power sometimes failed to provide a sturdy base for our own mere human responsibility and obligation. Each generation which inherits this creative tension between form and freedom, structure and flexibility, divine rulership and human response, may err toward legalism or antinomianism (a belief that the faith necessary for salvation does not involve obedience to the moral law), a bullying moralism, or an easy-going carnality. To say "everything is God" may create just as big a problem as believing "everything is man." Somewhere along the way, the Gospel stressed by the early Church and the fathers of the first three centuries was forgotten; man's ability to respond freely to God's dealings was lost, at first, theoretically, and later, practically. Forster and Marsden, in their definitive analysis of this problem, note:

"The doctrine of 'free will' seems to have been universally accepted in the early church. Not a single church figure in the first 300 years rejected it and most of them stated it clearly in works still existent.... We find it taught by the leaders of all the main theological schools. The only ones to reject it were heretics like the Ognostics, Marcion, Valentinus, Manes (and the Manichees), etc. In fact, the early fathers often state their belief on 'free will' in works attacking heretics." They then go on to summarize the main points of this consensus: (1) Rejection of free will is the view of heretics (2) Free will is a gift given to man by God—for nothing can ultimately be independent of God and (3) Man has free will because he is made in God's image and God has free will (Forster and Marsden, *God's Strategy In Human History*, p. 244).

It should be noted here that this stress on human freedom was not absolutely unbounded; man is only free so far. He was not free to save himself or to earn some kind of favor with God by good works outside of surrender to Christ. The early Church did not believe that man without God's help could do God's work, nor that His grace was given as we deserved. But, neither did they believe that faith itself was an "irresistible gift," or that human beings were not really free or able to reject or respond to God's Spirit. We can trace the genesis of this error historically to the fourth century and some of the philosophical speculations of Augustine. Some of the best of the early Reformers, anxious to guard the Church from a *Pelagian*[1] works-righteousness and humanism, began instead to adopt a picture of God and a view of His rulership perilously close to fatalism. They began to not only believe God allowed evil in the world, some actually taught that He *willed* it; that all that happened was the result of God's express design and purpose, that *all* acts in the Universe could be ultimately traced to God's decree. Some went so far as to say in perfect seriousness, but faulty exegesis, that God created sin, that wrong was the express result of divine design, and that Satan, in acting as he did, was enacting the will of God! They concluded that the destiny of all men was fixed forever before birth by divine decree. If you were headed for hell it was, of course, your fault. And if God had not, for some reason, in His wisdom, seen fit to include you in His list of those chosen to demonstrate His mercy, Christ did not die for you

---

[1]Pelagian: One who denies the original sin and consequently believes that man has perfect freedom to do either right or wrong.

130

and God's only interest in your well-deserved future was to display His just wrath and vengeance. They said it fearlessly, courageously, but, to their credit, neither claimed to like it or understand it.

Now, in the kindly light of a progressive understanding of Church history, we can thank God for the good they accomplished without considering them or their teachings infallible. We must avoid one major consequence of this early extreme view: its practical stress on force rather than persuasion. Some came to believe that if the only will in the Universe was God's will, no creature could resist that coercive will. If all men were the way they were by the decree of God, then the elect of God (themselves changed without choice), were perfectly justified in using force on a human level to accomplish God's will. This explains, while it does not excuse, the violent, unjustifiable words and deeds of some of the early Reformers; they were, after all, only trying to be consistent with their theology. But God is merciful. He raised up other generations that moved the Church toward a more Christ-like understanding.

All our revivalists of the First and Second Awakenings, whether Calvinist or Armenian, believed and strongly practiced human responsibility. Some, like Whitefield, fearlessly preached Augustine's view of divine election as selection, trusting that those who responded were the elect, and those who did not were not. But, they did not let it hinder them from stressing, "Ye must be born again!" Others, like the careful and scholarly Wesley, were theologically opposite. Also in the highways and byways with the same Gospel, they were convinced instead that Christ died for all men and that "whosoever will may come." Neither side in revivals became locked into the kind of fatalism one church board of another time adopted, responding to a young shoemaker's offer to go overseas as a missionary with a: "Sit down, young man! When God wants to evangelize the heathen, He will do it without your help." William Carey did not "sit down." He went to India and became the father of modern missions. And if we learn anything from the first two awakenings, it is this—the Church has a real and significant role in the purposes of God. As Francis Schaeffer puts it, each choice significantly affects history. What you do in response to God can change your world forever. "If any man *will do His will* he shall know..." said the Lord Jesus (John 7:17). And "to *as many as received* Him, to them *gave He the power to become* the sons of God, even to them that believe on His name" (John 1:12).

(2) *Holiness Unto The Lord: Purity.*

The second great lesson restored to the Church in these awakenings was a more practical realization of the Church's understanding of *sanctification*. It was the major thrust of both Wesley and Finney, their chief concern next only to the glory of God and the salvation of souls. The "strangely warmed" heart Wesley embraced in his conversion experience at Aldersgate was translated into fire by the January 1st, 1739 Fetter Lane meeting, where he and his original band of Methodists called on God for power to live lives of holiness and effective service.

"Mr. Hall, Kinchin, Ingham, Whitefield, Hutchins and my brother Charles were present...with about sixty of our brethren. About three in the morning, as we were continuing instant in prayer, the power of God came mightily upon us, inasmuch that many cried out for exceeding joy and many fell to the ground. As soon as we were recovered a little from that awe and amazement at the presence of His majesty, we broke out with one voice, 'We praise Thee, Oh God, we acknowledge Thee to be the Lord'" (*Journals of John Wesley,* Vol. II, p. 125). It was after this that Wesley began to see much fruit. For him, the "three pillars of the church" were repentance, faith, and holiness.

Charles Finney not only met Christ, but he had his "mighty baptism in the Holy Spirit" the same day, an experience he later related as the key of power required to lead an effective and dynamic life of faith. Timothy Smith, in his excellent introduction to Finney's Oberlin Papers, comments: "Like John Wesley, Finney drew upon Moses and the prophets, but re-inforced that source by appeal to the long tradition of Puritan or covenant theology. Moreover his starting point was not Moravian pietism, but...the law of disinterested benevolence —what Wesley called perfect love" (Smith, *The Promise Of The Spirit,* p. 19). Early, in having to deal with what he saw as terrible apathy, fatalism, and irresponsibility in the Church, Finney laid such a stress on human responsibility and freedom "as to allow the charge that he ignored the role of God's grace" (Smith, *The Promise Of The Spirit,* p. 19). Later, however, in a way that was to profoundly affect both America and England, he began to preach that such grace, in the baptism of the Holy Spirit, was the key to the sanctification of both society and individuals. Christians could "partake of the divine nature—the moral attributes or perfections of God" by the Spirit, through the promises of Scripture; an inward holiness wrought by the Spirit of God, "the substance and spirit of the law written in the heart by the Holy Ghost" (Smith, *The Promise Of The Spirit,* pp. 18, 22).

(3) *The Work Of The Kingdom: Compassion.*

Another important link that had major consequences for the nations was the link between a genuine Christian life and the reformation of the world. Not until Moody's day did revivalists begin to give up on society. (The Scofield Reference Bible popularized an interpretation of prophecy that gave birth to an unfortunate "save all you can, but you can't stop a sinking ship" mentality.) On the contrary, all the early reformers and revivalists were united in their belief that the Lord held divine right to the deeds of society and all its disciplines. It was God's will to both bring back such fallen structures under His dominion and to re-establish Christ's Lordship in every area of life. It is a simple fact that John Wesley's Methodists did more to save England from what could have been the same bloodbath as the French Revolution than any other single factor of that century. Even earlier, though sometimes upheld in a more legal, Old Covenant way, this was the consistent theme of the Puritans and the early Reformers, as well as that of those who followed them, exploring the promises of the New Covenant. This was no ostrich head-in-the-sand approach to problems; they never believed living in a hole would make you holy. Again referring to Charles Finney's contribution, Timothy Smith says:

"Never a Pelagian, I think, Finney had found a way to reclaim the doctrine of God's sovereignty without becoming a Calvinist either. He had discovered, he believed in Scripture, a Pentecostal version of covenant theology that opened the way to an evangelical unity that Wesley and Whitefield sought but were never able to accomplish. Rooting the experience of the baptism of the Holy Spirit in the Old Testament covenant of holiness also insulated it against the anti-intellectual and mystical corruptions of it that Wesley feared and that, alas, forgetting Finney, twentieth-century Pentecostals seemed often to have embraced" (Smith, *The Promise of the Spirit,* pp. 22-23).

Until this last century, no Christians thought their task was to just "take care of your own lives and run up your bills for the Anti-Christ." The revivalists linked conversion and spiritual growth directly to the alteration of society. They had a grand and glorious vision of a mighty revival, perhaps spreading throughout the world in their day, to prepare mankind for the Second Coming of Christ who would return and set up His millennial Kingdom.

Smith sums up this key contribution best seen in the social dynamic loosed on society in the 1857 Revival as follows: "When Finney discovered, apparently out of his own study of the English Bible, the logical and historical links between the covenant promise in the Old Testament and Jesus' covenant promise in the New of His continuing presence through the sanctifying Comforter, the Holy Spirit, the circle was complete. He then proclaimed, as Wesley himself had only rarely declared, that the entire sanctification of the believer's moral will was achieved through the baptism of the Holy Spirit. That proclamation did not reduce but in fact radicalized Christian concerns for social justice. For it offered to Calvinist, Pietist and Armenian alike a way of repossessing the doctrine of the sovereignty of God over individuals as well as over the structures of society" (Smith, *The Promise Of The Spirit,* p. 19).

Finney and his friends and brothers of both Awakenings attempted to prepare the world for Jesus to live in again; they did not live to see it. But, their vision of society had much better immediate and long-term consequences than the dominant ones of our past few decades. As Lovelace points out from Moody's time on, prophesying our inability by divine decree to redeem society may have helped us lose it.

Again, we can find flaws in these men and women of God. Though much more evangelistic, compassionate, and certainly more Christ-like in practical character than some of the earlier saints, they did not live long enough to see a flowering of some of the

136

things they had begun to experience in their lives. Power to be free, power to live clean, and power to affect the world; they saw them all as the pillar of fire moved on. And, God is not finished. In the accelerating events of this century, He has restored still further facets of His awesome nature; supernatural power allowing Him due worship in spirit and truth, and His demonstrated power to heal a physically as well as morally sick world. Thus, we come to the next great point in history, one which sets the stage for the revivals of our twentieth century. The 1857 Revival laid the final groundwork of what some believe may be completed in your time, His last and greatest demonstration of His glory.

PART IV

The 1857 Revival

THE 1857 REVIVAL

Which comes first, revival or judgment? In the 1857 Revival, from which issued the awakenings in Ireland, Scotland, Wales, and England a year or two later, a near socio-economic collapse jolted America away from her apathy into a national cry for spiritual reality. Though in 1860 more than five million out of her thirty million people were Protestant church members, and around three million of these evangelical Baptists or Methodists, these numbers (like in our time) seemed to have little effect on the nation. For ten early years (1845-1855) America's spiritual life steadily fell apart. Dr. Orr lists five contributing factors (again, uncannily like our day) which led to a great economic collapse in the country:

(1) *Gain, gambling and greed.* Speculation, spectacular wealth, and prosperity for an elite few widened the gap between the have and have-nots, with a corresponding rapid increase in violent crime.

(2) *Occult domination.* A nation hungry for the supernatural turned to spiritualism which gained a popular foothold over many minds.

(3) *Immorality.* A Playboy philosophy of "free love" was advocated and accepted by many.

(4) *Commercial and political corruption.* Bribes, graft, and illegal business practices were ripe in the nation; national laws still legalized the cruel system

of slavery.

(5) *Atheism*, agnosticism, apathy and indifference to God, to the church and its message abounded on every hand. "The decline was four-fold; social, moral, political and spiritual" (Orr, *The Fervent Prayer,* p. 1).

And judgment came. Both secular and religious conditions combined to bring about a terrible economic and social crash; thousands of merchants were forced to the wall as banks failed and railroads went into bankruptcy. Factories shut down; vast numbers were thrown out of employment, New York City alone having 30,000 idle men. By October of 1857, people were no longer into speculation and gain, with despair and hunger staring them in the face.

In Hamilton, Ontario, Canada, Walter Palmer, a Holiness Methodist physician and his talented wife Phoebe (herself a firebrand preacher), began a series of meetings soon reported in a New York journal as an "extraordinary revival" with 300 to 400 converts. Walter and Phoebe, in common with many of Finney's converts of the era, were ablaze with a burning desire to implement the message of personal and social holiness, and from such a practical sanctification to extend the Kingdom of God throughout the whole earth.

Beginning with the premise, "God requires present holiness," and Finney's logic, "God would not require what we cannot do," Phoebe urged a complete consecration to God including spouse, children, possessions, reputation, and (for women)—the willingness to preach! From such an act of simple faith and corresponding testimony, she urged a present possession of holiness, rather than the life-long process of Wesley in his initial emphasis. Her preaching, teaching, half-a-dozen books, and her editing of *"The Guide to Holiness"* left "an indelible impact on both Methodism and the wider Church" (Nancy Hardesty, *Great Women of Faith,* pp. 88-90). Phoebe was already deeply involved in slum work, prison ministry, missions to the poor (The Five Points Mission), juvenile delinquent homes, orphanages (one for 500 black children), a ministry to the deaf, and the predecessor to the Y.W.C.A., the "Ladies Christian Union." Now the foremost Methodist advocate of Christian sanctification, she spread benevolent responsibility everywhere through home groups, camp meetings, and the churches. Here, the message of personal holiness and social righteousness found its greatest expression of power. Timothy Smith says in his "Revivalism and Social Reform": "A third and quite utilitarian impulse of the holiness revival, (was) the hunger for an experience which would 'make Christianity work.' Finney, the reformer, Mrs. Palmer, the pioneer of many benevolent and missionary enterprises, and William E. Boardman, organizer and executive head of the United States Christian Commission did not seem like mystic dreamers to their generation....they rang the changes on...the theme that the Spirit's baptism was the secret of pulpit power and the fountain of that energy which alone could accomplish the evangelization of the world" (Smith, *Evangelical Origins of Social Christianity,* p. 145). Later, the Palmers helped spread the message and fire to Great Britain, preaching there over four years. Eventually, some 25,000 people were reportedly converted, especially under Phoebe's ministry, with many more making committments to the "deeper life."

Only twenty-one people were saved when this Canadian revival began, but it grew steadily until anywhere from 20 to 45 were converted each day, with all classes kneeling at the altar, from little children to the city mayor. "Laity" leadership here was a key which became true of the whole later awakening. This initial notice was soon followed by increasing reports of local small awakenings in various states. In December of that year, a convention on revival was called by the Presbyterians; 200 ministers and many laymen attended, and much of the time was spent in prayer. Baptist and Methodist pastors in New York set aside a day a week for all-day intercession for an outpouring of the Spirit. By the New Year, messages were preached all over the East on revival.

Prayer was such a key in this 1857 Awakening that it has been called *"The Prayer-Meeting Revival."* God laid a call on Jeremiah Lamphier, an upper New York born businessman converted in 1842 during a revival in the Broadway Tabernacle built by Finney a decade earlier. Seeing the terrible need in the city for God, he gave up his business in order to be a city street missionary. With social collapse staring the city in the face, Lamphier walked the streets, passing out ads for a noon-day prayer meeting to be held Wednesday at the Dutch Church on the corner of Fulton Street in downtown New York. For 5, 10, 15, 20, 25 minutes he waited alone, his faith tried. But then, at 12:30, six men came in, one after another. The next week, there were twenty; by the first week in October they had decided to meet daily instead of weekly. Within six months, over 10,000 businessmen were meeting every day in similar meetings, confessing sin, getting saved, praying for revival. Most of the organizers of the prayer meetings were businessmen; people had meetings in stores, company buildings, and churches. With hardly an exception, churches worked together as one, with no time for jealousy. By common consent, doctrinal controversies were left alone.

America began to live again. In just two years, over a million converts were added to churches of all denominations. The social and ethical effects continued for almost half a century. Geographically, the blessing spread to Great Britain which had over 27 million people, of whom a third attended State and Free Church services. It first touched Ireland, then Scotland, Wales, and finally England. There were 100,000 converts in Ulster, 100,000 additional in Wales, 300,000 in Scotland, and more than half a million in England by 1865 (300,000 joined Methodist, Baptist, and Congregational churches). Over a million converts were ultimately added to the churches of Great Britain.

Some of the great ministries of more recent history developed during this awakening. The revival saw the flowering of the ministry of *D.L. Moody* and *Ira Sankey*, the world-changing influence of *William and Catherine Booth* and the Salvation Army, *Hudson Taylor's* revival-based concept of interdenominational missions, the China Inland Mission, which in due time became the largest Protestant or Catholic missionary body. A large number of philanthropic societies developed and prospered, concerned enough about the hurt and lost and unwanted to care for children, reclaim prostitutes and drunks, and rehabilitate criminals. City Missions expanded evangelism into theatres, open-air meetings, slum visitations; the Open Air Mission, founded in 1853, flowered under evangelistic teams directed by Gawin Kirkham (Orr, *The Fervent Prayer,* p. 120-127). The Awakening was primarily an urban rather than a rural movement. The "English-speaking world fast becoming one of ever-enlarging cities with huge concentrations of population that had left forever the influence of rural churches behind" (Orr, *The Fervent Prayer,* p. 128).

One of the first effects of the revival was a new and intense sympathy for the poor. "God has not ordained," protested *Anthony Ashley Cooper* (Lord Shaftesbury), "that in a Christian country there should be an overwhelming mass of foul, helpless poverty" (Orr, *The Second Evangelical Awakening,* p. 99). As a boy of fourteen, he watched with horror as a drunk burial party, shouting a lewd song, dropped the coffin of the pauper they were carrying to burial. The drunks fell in a heap in front of him cursing and swearing. "Good heavens!" he muttered, "can this be permitted because a man is poor and friendless?" From that day on, this teenager (who would grow to become a tall, young aristocrat, full of fun and life, and described by one woman as "the handsomest man I ever saw") purposed to give his life to the poor and oppressed. He wrote in his diary at 26: "Time was when I could not sleep for ambition. I thought of nothing but fame and immortality. But I am much changed. I desire to be useful to my generation, and die in the knowledge of having advanced true happiness by having advanced true religion." He faced terrible times and conditions, and fought for justice with tireless, passionate determination. Children "sometimes four or five, but generally between seven and thirteen were shipped by bargeload" to other cities to do the work of men, bound by "apprenticeship" until they were 21. And, completely at the factory owner's mercy, they were employed at cotton mills thirteen, fourteen, fifteen or even sixteen hours a day; during rush periods sometimes twenty-four hours a day with only half an hour off for dinner. Their whip-wielding overseers paid by each child's output" (Garth Lean, *Brave Men Choose,* p. 45).

Lord Shaftesbury attacked terrible social evils such as these and many others like them in public and in Parliament; to those "who said of London's 30,000 naked, wandering, homeless children 'what will you do with them when educated?' he replied 'What will you do with them if left where they are?' " (Lean, *Brave Men Choose,* p. 46). These industrial conditions he fought and suffered over were the same ones observed by another would-be world changer, who for 34 years lived within a few miles of him, and was also in London during the years of the great revival—*Karl Marx*. With a sister-in-law active in the evangelical Lower Rhineland Revival which accomplished some tremendous social improvements while Marx was growing up in Germany, he was certainly not ignorant of Christian things. The sad thing was that Marx lost three of his own children through malnutrition during his early years in London. He blamed it on the failure of a "sneaking and hypocritical" Christianity to change the system, and with Engels (whose family was part owner of one of the cotton mills), he set out to destroy it and everything around him. Bitter, covered in boils, and full of hate, he sat in the British Museum writing "Das Kapital" when Moody came to London to preach. He hated Christians, not because he failed to see any real power to transform society, but because of his own counterfeit conversion, and subsequent failure. He believed they had to be, like himself once, nothing but self-deceived hypocrites. Having already written off Christianity, Marx now had nothing but spite for their doing good, and in this way delaying the day of violence which would usher in his own proud and perverse dream of a new world in his image. Christian meekness, humility, steadfastness, obedience, and kindness he put down as cowardice, self-contempt, abasement, and slavish subjection. It must have been hard to live with his rage when a godly revolutionary like Shaftesbury contradicted Marx's false assumption every day. Later, Marx's disciples were to confront another awesomely holy radical in the person of Catherine Booth, whose own fiery spiritual and practical attacks on corrupt society disturbed them so much that to this day the Salvation Army is the only religion officially banned in the Soviet Union.

Shaftesbury, believing "what is morally right cannot be politically wrong and what is morally wrong cannot be politically right" (Lean, *Brave Men Choose*, p. 48), originated more Royal Commissions of social investigation than any Parlimentarian in all British history—extending benefits to all classes of working people—pushed through more change than Marx ever did, and eventually earned the beloved nickname "The People's Earl." The Hammonds, economic historians critical of his entire approach, nevertheless admitted the relevance of his social reforms: "He did more than any man or government to check the power of the new industrial system" (Lean, *Brave Men Choose*, p. 39).

Nor were Shaftesbury or Booth the only ones of social compassion. *Tom Barnado*, the youngest of a brilliant Dublin family, after attempting to explain away examples of conviction as "emotional hysteria," became a Christian and founded the famous Dr. Barnado Homes in London's tragic East End and later throughout the whole country. George Mueller's orphanage had of course been in operation many years, keeping up to 10,000 children happy and alive through his work of faith. But something more needed to be done for young working people.

George Williams, converted at 16 one Sunday winter evening in 1837, launched the Teen Challenge of his generation, the Young Men's Christian Association (Y.M.C.A.) on June 6th, 1844. He, with some of his new converts, had "looked with deep concern and anxiety upon the almost totally neglected spiritual condition of the mass of young people engaged in the pursuit of business. . . we regard it to be a sacred duty, binding upon every child of God to use all the means in his power and to direct all his energies in and out of season toward the promotion of the Saviour's Kingdom and the salvation of souls" (J.E. Hodder Williams, *The Life Of Sir George Williams,* p. 114). Two men's messages helped give him heart for this vision; *Finney* of America and *Binney* of England! Williams was deeply stirred to evangelism, revival, and prayer through Finney's *Lectures on Revivals* and *To Professing Christians* which he gave out to his new converts. He was also highly influenced by the English preacher Thomas Binney who preached stirring, contemporary sermons against cant and hypocrisy, calling on young men to rise up and do battle for character and honest work. "Probably no man of his time developed so preeminently in the pulpit the tendency of the thinking and reading of the age. (Binney) preached the reality of the battle that is life, and as he pictured it, the fight was glorious, the victory sure" (Williams, *The Life of Sir George Williams,* p. 38). The Y.M.C.A., helped by men like D.L. Moody, reached out both in the U.S. and Britain and mobilized thousands of young men for evangelism.

Men like *David Livingstone* held out the challenge for Africa during the revival; *Mary Slessor,* converted in Dundee in 1860, joined the United Presbyterian mission in Nigeria and did extraordinary work among the tribes. The seed of the *Keswick Conventions*[1] of London, Oxford, and Brighton in 1873-5 was laid by *Evan Hopkins,* a newly-converted young clergyman, who had read William Edwin Boardman's hugely successful treatise, *The Higher Christian Life,* published in 1860 at the height of the Awakening. He joined with *Canon Harford Battersby* (active in the Carlisle Awakening) to begin the conventions which gained a unique leadership position in the Christian world. A majority of its leaders were either evangelists or converts of the Revival. Henry Varley ministered there; D.L. Moody, Reuben Torrey, A.J. Gordon, A.B. Simpson, J. Wilbur Chapman, and Handley C. G. Moule all supported it or spoke there; Andrew Murray and F.B. Meyer became its public voice. In Britain, Armenians and Calvinists got along well together over Boardman's writings, discussing differences "Fraternally"; but in the United States, holiness churches splintered in debate and "heated defense" over opposition from church officials, fanaticism, and attacks on Holiness doctrine, a situation that sadly persisted for 100 years.

---

[1]Keswick Conventions: Famous "deeper life" teaching conventions.

D.L. MOODY
1837-1899

As Finney dominated American evangelism in the middle third of the 19th century, the stout, simple, and sincerely affectionate D.L. Moody did so for the final third, more than forty years after the initial awakening, until 1904 and the outbreak of World War I. His Sunday School, started in 1858 in a vacant saloon, became the largest in Chicago, and eventually a church. By 1860, he had given up his shoe business ($5,000 a year) to "live by faith" ($150 for the first year!). In 1864, with his own building on Illinois St., he was elected Chicago President of the Y.M.C.A. There, he met two little old ladies, Mrs. Sarah Cooke and Mrs. Hawxhurst, who joyfully interceded for his spiritual lack: "We have been praying for you... You need power!" "I need power! Why I thought I had power.... They poured out their hearts that I might receive the anointing of the Holy Ghost. There came a great hunger in my soul. I knew not what it was. I began to cry as never before. The hunger increased. I really felt that I did not want to live any longer if I could not have this power for service" (Edman, *They Found The Secret,* p. 83).

In 1871 (a night he did not finish with an invitation), a $200,000,000 tragedy struck; the great fire of Chicago burned fifty churches to ashes, laid to waste a third of the city, killed nearly 200 people, and left approximately 18,000 homeless. The fire had also destroyed the new Y.M.C.A. Farwell Hall had built at the cost of $200,000 three years earlier. Heartsick, Moody set out to raise funds for the homeless. While visiting New York in 1871 to fund-raise, and "crying all the time God would fill me with His Spirit," he had "such an experience of His love that I had to ask Him to stay His hand" (Edman, *They Found The Secret*, p 84). After this baptism in the Holy Spirit, he began powerful evangelistic meetings with Ira D. Sankey, whom he had met the year before. "The sermons were not different; I did not present any new truths; and yet hundreds were converted. I would not now be placed back where I was before that blessed experience if you should give me all the world!" (Edman, *Deeper Experiences Of Famous Christians*, pp. 83-84).

The next year, he visited Britain again and was startled to hear the Australian, Henry Varley, say, "Moody, the world has yet to see what God will do with a man fully consecrated to Him" (J.C. Pollock, *Moody*, p. 99). Moody went back to Chicago for Sankey, and in June, 1873, both families moved to Liverpool to "win 10,000 souls" by invitation of the Anglican clergyman, William Pennefather. When they arrived, Pennefather was dead; they began any-way. Crowds gradually increased from place to place, until by Edinburg they not only had the peo-ple's enthusiastic approval but "after careful study, the minister's unreserved backing." He introduced the noon-day prayer meeting of the 1857 Revival again; evening meetings were jammed, crowding the largest auditoriums. From there, they preached in Dundee, Glasgow (thousands were converted), Belfast in the fall of 1874 (again several thousand converted); and in Manchester, Sheffield, and Birmingham, each with growing success. Finally, they preached in London, climaxing with 20,000 people nightly in the Agricultural Hall at Islington. William Taylor of California continued these meetings while Moody moved on to preach to the poor in Bow by day and the rich in the Haymart Opera House each evening. These meetings lasted 20 weeks and attracted 2,500,000 people.

Out of Moody's 1882 Cambridge University meetings, of which Moody said, "There never was a place I approached with greater anxiety. . . . Never having had the privilege of a University education, I was nervous about meeting University men," came wonderful results from what initially seemed a disaster (Pollock, *Moody,* pp. 228-229). Seventeen hundred people noisily crowded into a hall that first evening to hear the hick American evangelist who could somehow say "Jerusalem" in only two syllables, and, funnier still, didn't know any different. They "drowned out 70 brave undergraduates who tried to join in the hymns with vulgar songs." They yelled "Hear, hear" to Vicar John Barton's opening prayer, shouted derisive "Encore!" to Sankey's solo, and greeted Moody's one-syllable pronunciation of "Daniel" by "bringing down the house with cheering, jeering, clapping and stamping" (Orr, *Campus Aflame,* p. 90). Yet, Moody bravely hung in there. Only a hundred came the next night, but one was

Gerald Lander of Trinity College who (so embarrassed by the "civilized" behavior of his colleagues the previous night) apologized to Moody. God deeply touched Lander; he later became Bishop of Hong Kong. Over half of the audience responded to Moody's appeal that night. The next night, a hundred or more waited behind for counsel. The final meeting drew 1,800 and launched a worldwide interdenominational movement. Handley Moule, kneeling beside Moody on the platform, heard him say, "My God this is enough to live for" (Pollock, *Moody,* p. 239). C.T. Studd was the toast of the nation, captain of their champion cricket team, England's top sportsman, and inheritor of a small fortune. His brothers wrote to him about Moody's challenge, and out of this eventually came the "Cambridge Seven." This group consisted of either Moody's helpers or his converts, who toured universities and challenged students for missions. Studd gave up his cricket and gave away his fortune; large sums to Booth, Moody, and George Mueller's orphanages. His wife, not to be outdone by her husband's devotion, sold all their wedding presents! Together with other "holy madmen," they launched out to redeem another generation of spiritual warriors from the ranks of what he called the "Chocolate Soldiers," who melted and ran when the heat was on. Studd took as his motto: "If Jesus Christ be God and died for me, no sacrifice I make can be too great for Him" (McDonald, *True Discipleship,* p. 60).

What do we learn from this third great awakening

in the U.S. and Britain? Surely this: true revival changes the "moral climate of a community"; when God finds someone with the courage to pray, preach, and live a life before Him of holiness and compassion, He can literally change the face of a nation. What was needed was neither the recognition nor ordination of man. What really counted was the touch and the hand of God on ordinary people who were "wholly consecrated to Him."

PART V

The New Century Awakening

1904-1912

THE NEW CENTURY AWAKENING
1904-1912

Without a doubt, one of the most awesome moves of the Holy Spirit was the international outpouring at the turn of the twentieth century. Only in the past few decades have scholars been able to accurately assess just how widespread and powerful it was. Perhaps, until recently, it was the greatest world-wide manifestation of God in history. J. Edwin Orr, one of the first to research and realize the immense extent of this harvest, notes that "the first manifestation of phenomenal revival occurred simultaneously among Boer prisoners of war in places 10,000 miles apart as far away as Bermuda and Ceylon. Missionaries and national believers in obscure places in India, the Far East, Africa and Latin America seemed moved at the same time to pray." Another significant fact for our day: As true today in the 1980's of the West as it was in the 1890's, most of them had "never seen or heard of it happening in mission fields, and few had witnessed it at home. Their experience was limited to reading of past revivals" (Orr, *Evangelical Awakenings,* p. 41).

This prisoner of war work was marked by "extraordinary praying, faithful preaching, conviction of sin, confession and repentance with lasting conversion and hundreds of enlistments for missions," and spread to an economically depressed

South Africa. Near the same time, awakening began in Japan with "unusual prayer, intensive evangelism and such an awakening of Japan's urban masses to the claims of Christ" that "Japanese churches almost doubled within the decade" (Orr, *Evangelical Awakenings In Eastern Asia,* pp. 13-14). Four years later, when Japan was involved in a momentous war with Russia, it would have been impossible.

Nor was it confined to Europe, Africa, and Asia. R.A. Torrey and Alexander saw the most fruitful meetings ever held in Australia and New Zealand. These South Pacific awakenings began launching worldwide evangelistc campaigns. A "Mission of Peace" by the Salvation Army convert, evangelist Gypsy Smith, to war-sick South Africa touched off an awakening in the population. Worldwide prayer meetings intensified (Orr, *Evangelical Awakenings,* p. 114).

But, the best-known and farthest-felt happening of the New Century decade was undoubtably the Welsh Revival. "With less than a score of intercessors when it burst, the churches of Wales were crowded for more than two years; 100,000 outsiders were converted, drunkenness was cut in half, many taverns went bankrupt. Crime was so diminished that judges were presented with white gloves signifying there were no cases of murder, assault, rape or robbery or the like to consider. The police became 'unemployed' in many districts" (Orr, *Evangelical Awakenings,* p. 114). Coal mines stopped work with transport difficulties. The pit ponies didn't understand their instructions; they couldn't recognize their owner's "cleaned-up" language! At least 80% of the converts were still true after five years, and those converts not killed in World War I lasted until well into the 1930's. Orr comments that the World War slaughtered a high proportion of those revived or converted, and left a dearth of men in the churches. Then, coal mines were hit by unemployment which continued into the 1930's Depression. As the revival took Scripture knowledge for granted, and preaching, deemed superfluous, was at a minimum, the next generation (only babies during the War years) was not ready for a later onslaught of anti-evangelicalism which captured a generation of otherwise disillusioned Welshmen for Marxism (Orr, *Evangelical Awakenings,* p. 115). "There arose another generation after them, which knew not the Lord" (Judges 2:10).

Yet, this Welsh outcropping of glory affected all nations. "Thirty English bishops declared the revival after one of their number, deeply moved, told of confirming 950 new converts in a country parish church. Other Protestant churches equal in membership there gained around 300,000 converts, bringing renewed obedience to the four great social commandments, reducing crime, promoting honesty, truthfulness and chastity" (Orr, *Evangelical Awakenings In Southern Asia,* p. 106). It swept Ireland, Scotland; under Albert Lunde, a great revival in Norway affected Sweden, Finland, and Denmark. Lutherans there called it "the greatest movement of the Spirit since the Vikings were evangelized." It broke out in Germany, France, and other

161

countries of Europe marked by prayer and confession. And, though not really much noticed until recently, it *reached out* (just as Evan Roberts had predicted) and affected the world.

India in 1905-1906 saw awakening in every province, with meetings in many places five to ten hours long. And, the Christian population jumped 70%, sixteen times faster than the Hindu population. In 20 years, pupils in Christian schools in India doubled to 595,724; 90% of all nurses were Christian, mostly trained in mission hospitals. Amy Carmichael recorded some of the effects among the rescued "devadasis," the little temple prostitutes she was ministering to in Dohnavur. On October 22nd, to quote one of the little girls, "Jesus came to Dohnavur." At the close of a morning service, she was obliged to stop, overwhelmed with the sudden realization of the inner force of things. It was impossible even to pray. "It was so startling and dreadful—I can use no other word—that details escape me. Soon the whole upper half of the church was on its face on the floor, crying to God, each boy and girl, man and woman oblivious of all others. The sound was like the sound of waves or strong wind in the trees.... The hurricane of prayer continued for over four hours. 'They passed like four minutes'; for the next two weeks they gave themselves to the Word and prayer; counseling around the clock. Almost the whole compound got saved; it deeply affected the village" (Orr, *Evangelical Awakenings In Southern Asia,* p. 133).

In Burma, Southeast Asia, the same year the

A.B.M.U. (American Baptist Missionary Union) baptized 2,000 of the Karens (tribe people), a single church baptized 1,340 of the Shans in December alone. Don Richardson's *Eternity In Their Hearts*, a significant study of God's dealings with hidden peoples untouched by missionary movements, makes for some mind-blowing reading. It gives us some keys to the spiritual roots of this area's awakening.

During the previous century, Adoniram Judson, the American Baptist missionary of 1817, had only one Buddhist convert in seven years' hard labor. Not surprisingly, he did not feel too effective in his missionary calling, and gave himself more to Bible translation. Yet, in his city, another untouched people called the Karens passed his door each day sometimes singing to One they called "Y'wa—the true God." One day, Ko Thah-byu, a Karen ex-robber and murderer came to Judson's house looking for work. During Christian instruction by George and Sarah Boardman, Judson's helpers, the Karen seemed spiritually dense until they began to teach him about the Bible. Astonishingly, the Karen recognized the legendary "lost book" telling about his own people's unknown God "Y'wa" which he believed had arrived in Burma! Full of excitement and destiny, the Karen became a prophetic evangelist, and eventually entire Karen villages would respond to his ministry. By 1858, there were tens of thousands of Karen Christians, all missionary-minded. They went in turn to their neighbors, the Kachin, and within the next century some 250,000 Kachin were converted!

In the 1890's, William Young saw the same thing happen again among the Lahu people, located near the Ivory Coast, with tens of thousands converted. Finally some disciples of Pu Chan, a local witch doctor of the head-hunting Wa, a tribal people, were led supernaturally to follow on a 200 mile journey to find the "lost book of God." Their journey ended in a missionary compound in the city of Kengtung where William Young was digging a well. "Hello," he said in Shan to the awed Wa disciples, staring down at this white-faced stranger. "May I help you?" When he held up his Bible and answered "Yes" in response to their trembling "Have you brought a book of God?", they fell at his feet, overcome with emotion, and immediately urged him to leave. Young, already with thousands of Lahu to teach, instead made a place for them to stay and train. The Youngs and their Karen converts, in addition to baptizing some 60,000 Lahu, soon found themselves with another 10,000 baptized Wa converts, who in turn spread the Gospel still further in Eastern Burma and Southwestern China.

Finally, across the border, the Englishman, James Outram Frazier of the China Inland Mission, having discovered the Lisu tribe, learned their language and crossed the border into Burma to see what he could learn about cross-cultural communication from the American missionaries. There, instead, he found a Baptist outpost occupied by Karen missionaries; and they sent him a Karen helper who learned to speak Lisu. Similar traditions of a "white-faced helper" who would restore a long-lost "book of

God" ushered in another awesome movement bringing tens of thousands of Lisu Chinese into the Kingdom (Don Richardson, *Eternity In Their Hearts,* pp. 74, 85, 89-100).

All this opened the door to what happened in India later in the 1900's and to the recent revival among the Nagas today. Few Christians know that two entire states of predominantly Hindu India—Nagaland and Mizoram—boast a higher per capita ratio of baptized Christians than any other area of equal size anywhere in the world! Churches in Nagaland (1,000,000 people) embrace 76% of the population. Mizoram counts 95% of her population as members.

The revival hit *Korea* in three waves 1903, 1905, and 1907—quadrupling the membership of the churches in a decade, creating the national church from almost nothing, and rolling on into the 1980's. Located in Seoul today are two of the largest churches in the world.

Jonathan Goforth's ministry in *Manchuria* has been recorded, but the extent of the China Awakening between the Boxer Uprising and the 1911 Revolution has not been comprehended. Yet, the number of Protestants doubled in a decade to a quarter million, twice that figure for the entire evangelical community. Missionaries pioneered secondary and higher education and laid the foundation of medical service.

In *Indonesia*, the 100,000 Evangelicals in 1903 tripled in a decade to 300,000. In subsequent movements of phenomenal power, one little island alone

(Nias) won more than that, converting two-thirds of the population. Later, in a small town on the island of Timor, in 1965, four nights before an attempted Communist coup, God sovereignly began to pour out His Spirit. The coup was averted, and in the subsequent anti-communist reaction, evangelistic teams went all over the islands with miracle ministries, reported as both healing the sick and raising the dead. In this Indonesian revival, water was reported turned to wine, food multiplied, men ate poison without harm, and walked across a river 30 feet deep. The 30,000 members (recorded in 1961) of the churches in central Java jumped to more than 100,000 almost doubling annually, and the Indonesia Bible Society found it impossible to keep up with statistics.

Latin America saw real inroads in Brazil and Chile during the opening of the twentieth century, preparing the groundwork for what took place during the last few decades. In 1952, praying with Demos Shakarian and Oral Roberts in California, Tommy Hicks saw a vision of South America as a vast field of golden grain, and set out for Argentina in 1954. Substituting for T.L. Osbourne who had been invited for evangelistic meetings with President Peron's permission, Hicks began services on the 14th of April. Soon, 6,000 people were at the services; the healing of a boy with a leg brace on the first night led to widespread publicity, and soon the meetings had to be moved to the larger Huracan stadium (seating 100,000 people). Then, incredibly, it rose to a quarter of a million; some claimed aggregate attendance exceeded two million. The stock of available Gospel literature in Latin America was all but exhausted; over 22,000 Bibles and 26,000 New Testaments were sold, and at least half a million decision cards were taken by the multitudes pouring through the stadium gates. The effect "broke the back of evangelical resistance." Assembly of God churches alone multiplied ten-fold in ten years. Others ministering there later also saw greatly increased attendance. In 1957, Oswald Smith had a crusade in Buenos Aires supported by 300 churches, with attendances between 10-20,000 and reaching an aggregate of 200,000 with more than a thousand conversions. Peter Wagner approximates the resultant growth in Latin America evangelical Christians as: 50,000 in 1900; more than 1 million in 1930; 1940's two million; 1950's five million; 1960's ten million; 1970's twenty million.

The Edinborough World Missionary Conference recognized more progress made in all *Africa* in the first decade of the twentieth century than ever before. From 1903-1910, believers jumped from 300,000 to 500,000. The beginnings of African educational and medical services were due to its missionary impulse. But, the full impact was not felt until the later years, when in the next half-century phenomenal revival created amazing growth in the Christian population. Now, according to Barrett's monumental *World Christian Encyclopedia*, some 4,000 Africans are converted every day, three times that number growing up in Christian homes, with some African leaders aiming to see a majority of their nation converted.

It is phenomenal to see how widespread the turn of the century revival was. Both international and ecumenical, it touched all major nations, and "involved all major churches—Anglican, Baptist, Brethren, Congregational, Disciple, Lutheran, Methodist, Presbyterian, and Reformed, leaving, (as in the days of the Puritans, Wesley, Finney, and Moody) only the Roman Catholic and Greek Orthodox communities relatively untouched" (Orr, *Evangelical Awakenings In Southern Asia,* p. 105). Orr notes that, "only in the mid-twentieth century when their changing attitude to Scripture accompanied a changing attitude to dissent have these (latter) bodies been affected by evangelical movements" (Orr, *Evangelical Awakenings,* p. 105).

There were charismatic phenomena—uncanny discernment, visions, trances but no glossalalia in Wales; only in the aftermath of the India awakening (as in the converts of the Los Angeles revival at Asuza) were there outbreaks of the phenomena of "tongues" from which Pentecostalism spread widely.

When news of the coming revival reached America, huge conferences of ministers met in New York, Chicago, and other cities to discuss what to do when it began in the U.S. And, they met just in time. The Methodists in Philadelphia soon had over 6,000 new converts in trial memberships; the ministers in Atlantic City claimed there were only 50 adults left unconverted in a population of 60,000! Churches in New York City took in hundreds on a single Sunday:

one recording 286 new converts, of which 217 were adults, 134 men and 60 were heads of families.

Here are excerpts about the Azusa Street Awakening which took place in Los Angeles, California:

"At Pastor Bartleman's church, meetings are held every night, all day Sundays, and all night every Friday. There is no order of services, they are expected to run in the divine order. The blessed Holy Spirit is the executive in charge. The leaders, or pastors, will be seen most of the time on their faces on the floor, or kneeling in the place where the pulpit commonly is, but there is neither pulpit, nor organ, nor choir.

"A young lady, for the first time in one of these meetings, came under the power of the Spirit, and lay for half an hour with beaming face lost to all about her, beholding visions unutterable. Soon she began to say, 'Glory! Glory to Jesus!' and spoke fluently in a strange tongue. On the last Sabbath, the meeting continued from early morning to midnight. There was no preaching, but prayer, testimony, praise, and exhortation."

To continue, here is an extract from an article written by Pastor Bartleman which appeared in the *Way Of Faith* in 1907:

"We detect in these present-hour manifestations the rising of a new order of things out of the chaos and failure of the past. The atmosphere is filled with inspiring expectation of the ideal. But unbelief retards our progress. Our preconceived ideas betray us in the face of opportunity. They lead to loss and ruin. But the world is awakening today, startled from her guilty slumber of ease and death. Letters are pouring in from every side, from all parts of the world, inquiring feverishly, 'what meaneth this?' Ah, we have the pulse of humanity, especially in the Church of today. There is a mighty expectation. And these hungry, expectant children are crying for bread. Cold, intellectual speculation has had nothing but denials for them. The realm of the Spirit cannot be reached alone by the intellect. The miraculous has again startled us into a realization of the fact that God still lives and moves among us" (Bartleman, *Another Wave Of Revival,* pp. 99, 103).

The 1905 Awakening "rolled like a tidal wave" through the south, packing churches for prayer and confession, adding hundreds to membership rolls. First Baptist of Paducah added a thousand in two months; the old pastor died of overwork. In the Middle West, churches were suddenly flooded by great crowds of seekers. Every store and factory closed in Burlington, Iowa to let employees go to services of dedication and intercession. The mayor of Denver declared a day of prayer; by 10:00 a.m. churches were filled; by 11:30 almost all stores were closed. Every school closed. The Colorado legislature closed; 12,000 attended prayer meetings in downtown theatres and halls. The impact was felt for a year.

In the West, great demonstrations marched through Los Angeles streets. United meetings pulled crowds of 180,000; the Grand Opera House, in Los Angeles, was filled at midnight with winos and hookers seeking salvation. For three hours a day, business practically stopped in Portland, Oregon, bank presidents and bootblacks were all at prayer meetings, while 200 department stores closed by agreement from 11:00 to 2:00.

Orr records that church membership in seven major denominations jumped by 870,389 in 1906 alone; in five years it was two million and growing. This did not even include the Holiness or Pentecostal converts or younger denominations whose rate of increase was even greater. The largest U.S. denomination of those days, the Methodists, in review, declared that revival had "sparked the public conscience, overthrown corrupt officials, crossed party lines, and elected Governors, Senators, Assemblymen, Mayors, and District Attorneys of recognized honesty" (Orr, *Evangelical Awakenings,* p. 103). The people of Philadelphia "threw the rascals out" and put in a dedicated mayor. "A wave of morality went over the country, producing a revival of righteousness. Corruption in state and civic government encountered a set-back for a dozen years, and the country was committed in degree to civic and national integrity until new forces of corruption came back in the 1920's" (Orr, *Evangelical Awakenings,* p. 103).

Now, let's take an in-depth look at eyewitness reports of the *focus* of this early twentieth century awakening—the Welsh Revival under Evan Roberts.

EVAN ROBERTS

The Welsh Revival

What is it like in such a divine awakening? Again, a rare volume written during the time gives us on the spot reports of what was happening as God moved across the land. Here are actual British and American newspaper accounts of this awesome phenomena excerpted from *The Great Revival In Wales* collected and published by the Reverend S.B. Shaw (in Chicago of 1905:)

The "Methodist Recorder" Report:

"Wales is in the throes and ecstasies of the most remarkable religious revival it has ever known. It is nothing less than a 'moral revolution.' Already in five or six weeks the fire has spread to six or seven counties and bids fair find its way...into every parish in Wales.... What has largely contributed to the rapidity of the movement is the widespread publicity given to it in the press—both secular and religious. Every day for weeks past, the 'South Wales Daily News' and the 'Western Mail,' the two leading dailies of South Wales, have devoted three or four columns to reports of it.... The converts already number many thousands. Mr. Evan Roberts calculates that in the mining valleys of South Wales alone—there have been at least 10,000 conversions. And if we add to this the harvest gleaned in various other places north and south, the number cannot be far short of 20,000."

*Report in the "Rams Horn" on
"Evan Roberts' Call From God."*

"A wonderful revival is sweeping over Wales. The whole country, from the city to the colliery (coal mine) underground, is aflame with Gospel glory. Police courts are hardly necessary; bars and pubs are being deserted, old debts are being paid to satisfy awakened consciences, and definite and unmistakable answers to prayer are being recorded.

"The leader in this great religious movement is a young man twenty-six years of age, Evan Roberts. He was a collier boy, then an apprentice in a forge, then a student for the ministry. But all his life he has yearned to preach the Gospel. He is no orator, is not widely read. The only book he knows from cover to cover is the Bible. He has in his possession a Bible which he values above anything else he has belonging to him. . . . When working in the colliery, he used to take his Bible with him, and while at work would put it away in some convenient hole or nook near his working place readily at hand when he could snatch a moment or two to scan its beloved pages. A serious explosion occurred one day. The future Welsh revivalist escaped practically unhurt but the leaves of His Bible were scorched by the fiery blast. 'Evan Roberts' scorched Bible' is a familiar phrase among his friends." (The page which the blast struck was 2 Chronicles 6—where Solomon as a young man prays for revival!)

The report continues:

"Little more than a month ago Evan Roberts was unknown, studying so as to prepare for the Calvinistic Methodist ministry. Then came the summons, and he obeyed. He insists that he has been called to his present work by the direct guidance of the Holy Ghost. At once, without question and without hesitation, he was accepted by the people. Wherever he went, hearts were set aflame with the love of God."

Here is a vivid report by a newspaper representative:

"The scene is almost indescribable. Tier upon tier of men and women filled every inch of space. Those who could not gain admittance stood outside and listened at the doors. Others rushed to the windows where almost every word was audible. When at 7:00 the service began quite 2,000 people must have been present. The enthusiasm was unbounded. Women sang and shouted till perspiration ran down their faces, and men jumped up one after another to testify. One told in quivering accents the story of a drunken life. A working collier spoke like a practiced orator; one can imagine what a note the testimony of a converted gypsy woman struck when, dressed in her best, she told of her reformation and repentance. At ten o'clock the meeting had lost none of its ardour. Prayer after prayer went up...time and again the four ministers who stood in the pulpit attempted to start a hymn, but it was all in vain. The revival has taken hold of the people, and even Mr. Roberts cannot keep it in check. His latest convert is a policeman who, after complaining that the people had gone mad after religion so there was nothing to do, went to see for himself, and bursting into tears, confessed the error of his ways and repented."

A prominent member of a Newport Baptist Church declared that Evan Roberts had been praying for 13 months for that wave of revival to come. He related how the young man was turned out of his lodgings by his landlady who thought that in his enthusiasm he was possessed or somewhat mad. He spent hours preaching and praying in his room until the lady became afraid of him and asked him to leave.

It may be observed that the dominant note of the revival was prayer and praise. Another striking fact was the joyous and radiant happiness of the evangelist. It has been remarked that the very essence of Roberts' campaign was mirth. To the rank and file of church ministers, this was his most incomprehensible quality. They had always regarded religion as something iron-bound, severe, even terrible. Evan Roberts smiled when he prayed, laughed when he preached. "Ah, it is a grand life," he cried. "I am happy, so happy that I could walk on air. Tired? Never. God has made me strong. He has given me courage." He was a leader who preached victory and showed how it may be won—victory over the dull depression and gloomy doubt of our time. Is it surprising that followers flocked by the thousands to his banner?

A generation had risen that had not seen the arm of God working as it had done in 1849 and 1859. "Now, to all appearances, the revival has arrived and it has all the marks of previous great awakenings. Strong men are held in its grip; the Spirit of God stirs to their very depths whole neighborhoods and districts. There is a tumult of emotion, an overpowering influence and a conviction of sin that can only be attributed to Divine agency. Personal eloquence, magnetism, fervor or mental power do not account for it. The only explanation is the one which the evangelist gives—'it is all of God.' The revival seems to work especially among young people. Its form, which is that of prayer, praise and personal testimony, and its absence of method make it the most methodical expression of the emotions of young hearts aflame with the love of God" (*The Story Of The Welsh Revival*, pp. 5-6).

These characteristics of brokenness and praise dominated the awakening. When a man asked Evan if the revival would come to London, he smiled and said, "Can you sing?"

William T. Stead, the famous London editor of the *Pall Mall Gazette*, thought by some to be the most powerful man in Britain, visited the revival. Here are excerpts of his impressions when interviewed by the *London Methodist Times* on his return:

"Well, Mr. Stead, you've been to the revival. What do you think of it?"

"Sir," said Mr. Stead, "the question is not what I think of it, but what it thinks of me, of you, and all the rest of us. For it is a very real thing, this revival, a live thing which seems to have a power and a grip which may get hold of a good many of us who at present are mere spectators."

"Do you think it is on the march then?"

"A revival is something like a revolution. It is apt to be wonderfully catching."

It may be difficult to imagine the intense power and supernatural conviction that marked this revival. Later, the interviewer asked Stead:

"You speak as if you dreaded the revival coming your way."

"No, that is not so. Dread is not the right word. Awe expresses my sentiment better. For you are in the presence of the unknown. . . . You have read ghost stories and can imagine what you would feel if you were alone at midnight in the haunted chamber of some old castle and you heard the slow and stealthy step stealing along the corridor where the visitor from another world was said to walk. If you go to South Wales and watch the revival, you will feel pretty much like that. *There is something there from the other world. You cannot say whence it came or whither it is going, but it moves and lives and reaches for you all the time. You see men and women go down in sobbing agony before your eyes as the invisible Hand clutches at their heart. And you shudder.* It's pretty grim I tell you. If you are

177

afraid of strong emotions, you'd better give the revival a wide berth."

"But is it all emotion? Is there no teaching?"

"Precious little. Do you think teaching is what people want in a revival? These people, all the people in a land like ours are taught to death, preached to insensibility. They all know the essential truths. They know they are not living as they ought to live, and no amount of teaching will add anything to that conviction."

"Then I take it your net impressions have been favorable?"

"How could they be otherwise? Did I not feel the pull of that unseen Hand? Have I not heard the glad outburst of melody that hailed the confession of some who in very truth had found salvation? Of course it is all very much like what I have seen in the Salvation Army. And I was delighted to see that at last the Welsh churches are recognizing the equal ministry of men and women. . . . There is a wonderful spontaneity about it all, and so far its fruits have been good and only good."

"Will it last?"

"Nothing lasts forever in this mutable world . . . . But if the analogy of all previous revivals holds good, this religious awakening will be influencing for good the lives of numberless men and women who will be living and toiling and carrying on the work of this God's world of ours long after you and I have been gathered to our fathers" (Shaw, *The Great Revival In Wales,* p. 56).

George T.B. Davis' Report to America:

Thirty-Four Thousand Conversions in Wales:

"I have just returned from a two day visit to the storm center of the great Welsh revival which is sweeping over Wales like a cyclone, lifting people into an ecstasy of spiritual fervour. Already over 34,000 converts have been made, and the great awakening shows no signs of waning. . . . It was my good fortune to take two meals with Mr. Roberts and to attend three meetings he conducted.

"It was 9:45 when we reached the place and even at that hour there were scores of people seeking admission. But the gates were closed and guarded by policemen for the church was already packed to the doors.

"My first impression! How am I to describe it? . . . a room meant to seat about 700 people crowded to suffocation with about 1,500. Up in the gallery, a young lady—almost a girl—was standing, praying with such fervor as I had rarely if ever witnessed before. One hand was upraised and her tones were full of agonized pleadings; and though it was in Welsh, so that I could not understand a word she uttered, yet it sent a strange thrill through me. Then a young man arose and, with rapt upraised face, prayed as though he were in the presence of the Almighty. The entire atmosphere of the room was white-hot with spiritual emotion, and my chief thought was: 'This is a picture of what must have occurred in the early church in the first century of the Christian era.'

"A hymn was now started, and my attention was riveted on Evan Roberts, who stood in the pulpit and led the music with face irradiated with joy, smiles, and even laughter. What impressed me most was his utter naturalness, his entire absence of solemnity. He seemed just bubbling over with sheer happiness, just as jubilant as a young man at a baseball game. He did not preach; he simply talked between the prayers and songs and testimonies, and then rarely more than just a few sentences at a time.

"In appearance the young evangelist is of medium height, slender, brown-haired. He is extremely nervous in temperament, and his pallor showed the strain of the meetings on him." (This physical and spiritual strain was to later tell terribly on Roberts' health.)

The young reporter then asked Evan for a message for America. He grasped his hand and gave him the following, amplified from the *Western Mail's* printed record of the essential message he was sharing then with the world:

"The prophecy of Joel is being fulfilled. There the Lord says, 'I will pour out My Spirit upon all flesh' (Joel 2:28). If that is so, all flesh must be prepared to receive. (You desire an outpouring of the Holy Spirit in your city? You do well. But remember, four conditions must be observed. They are essential.) Roberts continued:

"(1) *The past must be clear*, every sin confessed to God, any wrong to man must be put right. (Have you forgiven everybody—*everybody?* If not, don't expect forgiveness for your sins. Better offend ten thousand friends than grieve the Spirit of God—or quench Him.) (2) *Everything doubtful* must be removed once and for all out of our lives. (Is there anything in your life you cannot decide whether it is good or evil? Away with it. There must not be a trace of a cloud between you and God.) (3) *Obedience,* prompt, implicit, unquestioning, *to the Spirit of God* (At whatever cost, do what the Holy Spirit prompts without hesitation or fear.) (4) *Public confession of Christ.* (Multitudes are guilty of long and loud *profession. Confession* of Christ *as Lord* is of recent date. We also forget there is a Trinity in the Godhead and that the Three Persons are on absolute equality.... Is not He (the Holy Spirit) ignored entirely in hundreds of churches? Hear the Word of the Lord: 'Quench not the Spirit' [1 Thessalonians 5:19]. That is the one way to revival.) When the fire burns it purifies. And when purified you are fit to be used in the work of God. Christ said, 'And I, if I be lifted up from the earth, will draw all men to Me' (John 12:32). There it is. Christ is all in all."

"In the afternoon meeting while describing the agony of Christ in the Garden of Gethsemane. He broke down and sobbed from the pulpit; scores in the building wept with him. It had been announced to begin at 2:00 but before 12 the building was packed.... The air was stifling but the people minded it not a whit. They had forgotten the things of earth and stood in the presence of God. The

181

meeting began about noon and went on at white heat for two hours before Mr. Roberts arrived, ending at 4:30 p.m." (Shaw, *The Great Revival In Wales,* p. 62).

What was the revivalist like close-up in a meeting like that? David Matthews records: "There came a sudden calm. Hearing a movement behind me in the pulpit I looked up. Evan Roberts was on his feet. Our eyes met for a few seconds. I solemnly avow that those eyes searched through and through. They burned like coals of fire. In a split second my innermost soul seemed to be laid bare. I feared and shook . . . . Had there been a cover nearby, I most assuredly would have sought it" (Matthews, *I Saw The Welsh Revival,* p. 25).

Thus it was for glorious year after year, with some churches open twenty-four hours a day and producing incredible effects on the world. Before it began, Evan Roberts was a young man consumed with compassion over a world with no one to weep for it; God gave him a vision of a revival that would go around the world. Yet, Evan himself may never have known that that promise to him had been literally fulfilled. Only recently have we realized just how wide, how powerful, and how far-reaching this revival was. Roberts himself could never have seen the results we now know; all he had for his life's ministry was what God showed him one night as a young college student beside his bed in agonizing prayer. In a conversation with Syd Evons, who married Evan Roberts' sister, Mary, Roberts related the experience. After midnight, Roberts was walking with holy light on his face.

"Evan, what has happened to you?"

"I had a vision of all Wales being lifted up to heaven. The Holy Spirit is coming—we must get ready. We must have a little band and go all over the country preaching." He stopped and looked into his friend's face with piercing eyes.

"Do you believe God can give us 100,000 souls now?"

Perhaps Roberts thought he might be the one to carry the revival afar; perhaps he believed that, like Whitefield and Moody, he might travel from a revived British Isles to other continents, carrying the message which reached such astonishing focus in Wales. But, it was not to be.

What happened to Evan Roberts?

A question perhaps that will never be satisfactorily answered in this world. Long after the awakening had begun to spread through the British Isles, a nationally famous Welsh preacher, Peter Price, publicly criticized Roberts in print, after Evan's short and embarassingly unfruitful visit to his large and growing Dowlais Congregational Church. Some thought earlier that Price himself, with a mighty record of evangelism and outreach among the young, might be the natural choice of God to bring awakening to Wales before it came to Evan Roberts' town of Loughor. The young Roberts apparently faced "hardness" in his earlier meetings there; half-an-hour into Price's service, Roberts stood to deliver a scathing "word from the Lord" that someone "near him" was "blocking the way of revival" by criticism of both it and him, and that unless it was dealt with he would leave; he "would not take part in mock worship where the Holy Spirit was grieved." He left shortly after. (Matthews, *I Saw The Welsh Revival*, pp. 85-86).

Price's later letter to the *Western Mail* to correct "misconceptions" or "misconduct" he perceived in young converts of the revival also, unfortunately, resulted in his denouncing Roberts' work as false, shallow, and unreal, and his own work as genuine. This, physical strain, and a growing disunity Evan attempted to correct in some divisive breakaway works among the Northern churches led to one of the strangest endings of a ministry in history. Offered a retreat at the home of the godly Jesse Penn-Lewis and her husband, Roberts accepted and from then on never returned to ministry! The revival, of course, went on. It spread internationally, later deepened and developed into the teaching and instruction of the hundreds of thousands of converts it had generated. But, Evan Roberts effectively dropped completely and utterly out. He rejected all callers, ignored all letters, even refused to see his own concerned family, much to the embarassment of his hosts. Later, he co-authored, with Jesse Penn-Lewis, the controversial book *War On The Saints*. Attempting in this to describe the work of deception in the spiritual world, some think he may even have over-reacted by disavowing some of the genuine amongst the ever-present spurious incidents in the awakening. He simply vanished from the scene; perhaps in his own thinking, for the best. What was God's work, as he had always emphasized, after all would continue without him. And it did. He only emerged rarely after this at some public religious events, usually unnoticed and unheralded, and to all but a few who remembered, essentially forgotten.

PART VI

The Healing Revival

PIONEERS OF THE HEALING REVIVAL

Those first-generation Evangelists had eventually organized. "Western North Carolina and eastern Tennessee had *A. J. Tomlinson* and the Church of God, the Midwest had the Methodist, *Charles Parham. Azusa Street* was in 1906. By the end of World War II, the three largest churches were the *Assemblies of God*, the Church of God and the *Pentecostal Holiness Church.*" What set them apart from other fellowships was the central teaching of "the abiding possibility and importance of the supernatural element...particularly as contained in the manifestation of the Spirit" (Donald Gee, *Wind And Flame,* p. 3). Extending the stress of the Holiness Movement on personal holiness, or "entire sanctification," as an evidence of the indwelling Holy Spirit, Pentecostals "took this emphasis a step further in what some called a 'third work of grace' while others omitted sanctification and considered 'Baptism in the Spirit' the only subsequent experience to conversion" (Harrell, *All Things Are Possible,* p. 11).

Some had millennium vision. *Alexander Dowie,* the father of healing revivalism in America, built *Zion* in 1900 on 6,000 acres of land north of Chicago; by 1902, 10,000 people had moved there as the paradise for the righteous. "Out of Zion" came *F.F. Bosworth*, a band leader in Dowie's church who

189

moved to Dallas in 1910, pastored a strong independent church for ten years, and launched out on crusades. By 1924, there were reports of "some 12,000 that sought the Lord for salvation." Also from Zion was Dowie's protege, *John G. Lake,* who *W. T. Stead* called "the embodiment of the spirit of primitive Christianity" (*Adventures In God,* cover). Lake owed much to what he saw of Christ in the life of *W. J. ("Daddy") Seymour*, a black one-eyed preacher from Parham's Houston Bible school, who in the spring of 1906 felt led to move to California, there to receive a baptism of the Holy Spirit and play a major role in the Asuza Street revival. Seymour "had the funniest vocabulary," records Lake, "but there were doctors, lawyers and professors listening to the marvelous things coming from his lips. It was not what he said in words; it was what he said from his spirit to my heart that showed me he had more of God in his life than any man I had ever met up to that time. It was God in him who was attracting people" (Lake, *Adventures In God,* pp. 18-19). A year before leaving as a missionary to Africa, in prayer, John Lake received a vision of the various places where he would be and the extent of the spiritual work in each place. "I had faith to believe," he said, "that the thing God showed me would come to pass, and I have lived to see it through." For five years his African ministry, accompanied by wonderful miracles, stirred many. Andrew Murray said of Lake, "the man reveals more of God than any other man in Africa." With a scientific background himself, he even offered himself to a research clinic for testing.

(he wanted to see just how God healed), and often invited doctors to witness God's healing power directly during prayer (Lake, *Adventures In God*, pp. 18-31). Lake returned to pastor in Spokane, Washington, where, according to Gordon Lindsay, "100,000 healings were recorded in five years." And, his ministry resulted in the establishment of hundreds of churches.

Smith-Wigglesworth, along with Stephen and George Jefferies, was the best-known of the British Pentecostals. This "apostle of faith," once a British plumber and volunteer worker in Salvation Army missions, was a "commanding figure with twinkling small eyes in a stout face; rugged and refined at the same time, always dressed immaculately in a dark suit" (Hacking, *Smith-Wigglesworth Remembered*, p. 18). Always smiling, never without a Bible (the only book he ever read), he saw almost every kind of healing miracle in his ministry, including the raising of the dead. In common with other early healing revivalists, he was concerned for purity as well as power: "I want to move you," he said, "to a greater hunger for holiness and purity. The moment you look up when you are in a place of affection with Jesus the heavens are opened" (Hacking, *Smith-Wigglesworth Remembered*, p. 93). Glorifying Christ, honoring the work of the Holy Spirit, and anointing people with a custom-made little celluloid bottle of oil, he made several powerful evangelistic tours in the 1920's and 1930's. Stanley Frodesham said he "filled the biggest halls, ministered to record crowds and prayed for thousands" (Frodesham,

Maria B. Woodworth-Etter (born in 1844) of the United Brethren began an influential healing ministry in 1876 and later associated with the Methodist Holiness church, remaining active in revivalism until the 1920's. Her early life was marked by tragedies; she lost her drunkard father to a sunstroke when she was eleven, leaving her mother with eight children to provide for. Around sixteen, she married, and fighting a constant battle with sickness and ill health herself, she lost five of her six children. Tragedy cast her more on Christ. Broken and seeking only to know God's will, she received a call to ministry and battled her own prejudices over women's ministries, afraid of bringing reproach on Christ and ridicule from her friends and family.

Finally, accepting what God was obviously doing in her life, Maria launched out on a militant mission against sin in what some called "the most powerful seen in the twentieth century." "I felt impressed God was going to restore love and harmony in the church. I visited those disenting families; the third day of the meeting the trouble was all settled. All present came to the altar, made a full consecration and prayed for a baptism of the Holy Ghost and fire. That night it came. Fifteen came to the altar screaming for mercy. Men and women fell and lay like dead. I felt it was the work of God but did not know how to explain it or what to say. I was a little frightened . . . after lying for two hours all, one after another sprang to their feet as quick as a flash with shining faces and shouted all over the house. I had never seen such bright conversions or such shouting.... The ministers and old saints wept and praised the Lord...they said it was the Pentecost power, that the Lord was visiting them in great mercy and power" (*Maria Woodworth-Etter,* p. 37).

Another powerful woman evangelist of those days was the colorful and controversial *Aimee Semple McPherson.* She married *Robert Semple* in 1908, an Irish Pentecostal evangelist whose supernatural ministry had swept aside her youthful skepticism. She headed out with him, scared and expecting, to Macao, China. Shortly after he arrived, Robert caught a fatal disease, and all alone with her newborn little girl Roberta, Aimee returned to America. Remarrying Harold McPherson in 1912 with the stipulation that God's call to the ministry was first in her life, she had one child (Rolf) by him. Though at first content just to be a wife and mother, she came to feel she was avoiding her ministry; her health broke, and near death, she surrendered to the divine call. Earlier on, she was a tent evangelist. Later, after a disastrous fire in a wooden tabernacle in Durant, Florida, where a kerosene lamp blew up, she moved to Los Angeles, where fifteen years after Asuza Street the Pentecostal message was getting a good hearing. Her illustrated sermons, complete with Hollywood style special effects, "I want to speak on the last days of Pompeii next week," she told her crew, "and I need a volcano to erupt behind me," were the talk of California. But, above all, Aimee had a powerful attraction for the sick and the lost in her exceptional ministry of healing. To this day, people in Angelus Temple, her home church, can show you a room full of wheelchairs, crutches, and braces that people in her meetings had abandoned, instantly healed by the power of God. Her last authorized biography recounts her story of being kidnapped and the swirl of controversy it generated; Aimee was without doubt the most talked-about Christian woman of her time. She died on September 26, 1944, in Oakland, California. It was the same city where she had, 26 years earlier, received the vision of the "Foursquare Gospel," a denomination she founded which has now grown to 783 churches with 2,000 foreign mission stations, 32 day and Bible schools, and 117 daily or weekly radio broadcasts in the United States, Canada, and 27 other countries. The Foursquare Gospel Church has produced pastors and teachers of the spiritual caliber of the *Hayford brothers* (Jack and Jim) and *Jack Hamilton,* its present Bible College President.

Charles S. Price was probably the most influential of the post-World War II evangelists. Born in England with a law degree from Oxford, he imigrated to Canada as a young man, became a Methodist minister, and received the Baptism of the Spirit under Aimee Semple McPherson's ministry. In 1922, he launched out from his independent church in Lodi, California, to become a full-time evangelist; he died in 1947 shortly before the outbreak of the post-war revival, sensing in his spirit a growing cooperation among Christians. By 1943, a number of Pentecostal churches were able to join the *N.A.E.* (National Association of Evangelicals), the successor to the fundamentalist organization that had refused them in 1928. In 1947, American Pentecostals participated in a world convention in Zurich, and, in 1948, eight major churches formed the *Pentecostal Fellowship of North America*. David DuPlessis recorded, "the general effects of these international and national conferences have been noticed in city-wide and country-wide Union meetings held by Pentecostal evangelists. . .it is not uncommon to find from 5,000 to 10,000 and more. Such meetings were unheard of before the first World Conference of 1947" ("Voice Of Healing," July, 1965, p. 13).

THE HEALING REVIVAL
1947-1958

Time marched on. Many of the early Pentecostal pioneers passed on. Evangelicals had become more tolerant of the healing revival; after all not many of them had gone off into some fundamental doctrinal error, had been caught in immorality, or had absconded with the collection to South America. The financial situation for Pentecostals had also somewhat improved. They no longer had to live a hand-to-mouth existence on the sawdust trail. But, there was now a void; "The need of the hour was for leaders. Smith-Wigglesworth and Charles Price died within a few days of each other and fired many pure young hearts with a holy desire to pick up the torch of their ministry and carry it forward," wrote Donald Gee in 1956 (Gee, *Pentecost,* p. 17). The deaths of the pioneer evangelists, including Aimee Semple McPherson, left a void. Some troubled, older pentecostals wondered if the days of revival were over.

In fact, as David Harrell notes, "the great Pentecostal revival identified by some as part of the prophetic 'latter rain' was about to begin. The pioneers of divine healing revivalism were gone, but almost simultaneously with their passing, God raised up...many others to carry on a new wave of revival that has reached nearly every nation of the free world" (Harrell, *All Things Are Possible,* p. 30). It erupted in 1947 with "astonishing force." The practice of praying for the sick was "revived on a scale hitherto unknown" wrote historian John T. Nichol. DuPlessis said, "The sudden move toward mass evangelism has been just as unexpected and equally as little prepared for as the phenomenal growth ...fifty years ago. It cannot be attributed to anything else than the spontaneous move of the Holy Spirit upon all flesh" ("Voice Of Healing," July, 1965, p. 13).

That outburst from 1947 to 1952 was, at least numerically, an astonishing success. "Vast crowds have gathered in many places in the world," wrote Gee in 1956, that "far exceeded those of a former generation of evangelists" (Gee, *Pentecost,* p. 17). This set off a period of worldwide Pentecostal growth.

Perhaps the best-known evangelistic ministry amongst the evangelicals of the late 1940's was that of the dynamic young Southern Baptist, *Billy Graham.* With the advent of the nuclear bomb and the looming spectre of Communism on the horizon, America was gripped with a fear for her future. *Minister's Conferences* for revival prayer, such as those organized by *Armein Gesswein,* resulted in hundreds of missionaries, evangelists, and pastors from all denominations discussing revival in evening sessions often lasting long after midnight, with much confession and restitution.

Henrietta Mears' *Forest Home Conference* witnessed a number of outpourings of the Holy Spirit.

Influenced by the earlier writings and friendship of revivalists like J. Edwin Orr, Graham himself had a powerful experience with the Holy Spirit during one such visit to *Forest Home.* In a September 1949 Student Briefing Conference, where he preached with a ministry team to approximately 500 students, retreat topics taught were: *God and Students; Revival, the Work of God; How God Forgives Sins; The Searchlight of God; Sanctification; The Filling of the Spirit; and The Impact of Revival.* Later that year, in an historic series of meetings, he was led to preach the only message he ever repeated in the same crusade—*"How To Be Filled With The Spirit."* That eight-week campaign in Los Angeles, 1949, was "the spark that set revival fires burning across the nation"; key figures like *Louis Zamperini,* the Olympic runner, the singer and stage personality *Stuart Hamblen* and *Jim Vaus,* the notorious "wire-tapper" of organized crime became Christians; 350,000 people had been through the massive "tent cathedral" in 72 meetings and over 3,000 people had both professed conversion and come back to Christ. Newspapers, triggered by the newspaper magnate William Randolf Hearst's terse "Puff Graham," began to report the crusades that followed across the nation.

The fiery and articulate young evangelist bècame the figure-head, if not the spearhead, of hundreds of national crusades, prayer meetings for revival and renewed interest in outreach. Ministries like *Torrey Johnston's Youth For Christ* (in 1945 Graham was their first evangelist) attracted tens of thousands of high schoolers to their "rallies." An air of expectancy and urgency gripped evangelicals again. From that Los Angeles Crusade sermon, Billy summed up the dominant mood of the times:

"Everywhere I go I find that God's people lack something. God's people are hungry for something; God's people are thirsty for something.... I am persuaded that our desperate need tonight is not a new organization, nor a new movement, nor a method—we have enough of those. I believe the greatest need tonight is that our men and women who profess the name of Jesus Christ be filled with the Spirit.... I have asked God if there were ever a day when I should stand in the pulpit and preach without compassion and fire, I want God to take me home to heaven. I don't want to live. I don't ever want to stand in the pulpit and preach without the power of the Holy Spirit. It's a dangerous thing" (Graham, *Revival In Our Time,* pp. 105,108,119).

And it happened. That hunger for power broke out in the birth of a radically distinct stream from the more traditional evangelical responses. Their immediate ancestors of the early 1900's had claimed George Fox and his Quakers, John Wesley's early Methodists, the Plymouth Brethren, William Booth's Salvation Army, Asuza Street, and the holiness movement at the end of the nineteenth century as their roots. Scorned, laughed at, or ignored by many of the mainstream evangelicals, denied validity by an orthodoxy suspicious of fanaticism, false doctrine, and deception, they were criticized and denounced by psychiatrists, journalists, and medical doctors alike. Some were hated, spat on, even shot at. Religious leaders named them, in derision at first, "holy rollers" and "tongues-speakers." Eventually, seeing they were here to stay, they called them "Pentecostals." But, the best of these first pioneers of "latter rain" fasted, prayed, and paid a price to see through the ushering in of a significant restoration of spiritual power to the Church that has since been repeated in other countries around the world. From 1947 to 1958, many of these second generation Pentecostals were called *faith-healers* because they saw a revival of divine healing which launched the ministries of many independent evangelistic ministries.

David Harrell again comments: "In some ways the charismatic evangelists looked much like other revivalists in American history. They studied the techniques of figures such as Billy Sunday and Dwight L. Moody. They admired the success of Billy Graham. But they were not part of the same revivalistic stream—they were a sign-gifts-healing, a salvation-deliverance and Holy Ghost-miracle revival. Salvation from sin was preached, but whatever the intention of the evangelists, it was never the central theme of their meetings. All the gifts of the Holy Spirit, including speaking in tongues and prophesying, and all expressions of joy so common in pentecostal worship, were present in the early revivals but they were not the central theme. The common heartbeat of every service was the miracle ...when the Spirit moved to heal the sick and raise the dead" (Harrell, *All Things Are Possible,* pp. 5-6).

Gordon Lindsay, editor of the *"Voice of Healing,"*

became a teaching advisor and promoter of the revival with nearly fifty evangelists. A key figure of those times was the awesome and later terribly controversial *William Branham,* "an uneducated, timid and poorest of the poor Baptist evangelist" who, in 1933, at the age of 24, began to preach in Jefferson where over 3,000 people a night came to his meetings. In 1946 (after reportedly receiving an angelic visit and a commission for healing), he preached in the Jonesboro, Arkansas Bible Hour Tabernacle pastored by Rex Humbard's father. People gathered to the little city from 28 states and Mexico, with some 25,000 people attending! Unheralded by anything except his amazing gifts, Branham began to travel from city to city, creating astonishment and wonder wherever he went. A Shreveport pastor's daughter, seeing him arrive outside her house to begin meetings in her father's church, said: "All things we heard about him seemed quite incredible, but as he traveled southward he stopped with us. . . . Could I ever forget the first time I saw him that Sunday afternoon in 1947 when a little '38 Ford turned in our driveway, and a slight, tired man with the deep eyes of a mystic got out and looked around. As I watched from the window, I began to weep for no apparent reason, except that my heart seemed to break" (Anna Jean Price, "Voice Of Healing," November, 1955, pp. 9-10).

Under Lindsay's direction, Branham teamed with the colorful Canadian, *Ern Baxter*, in Vancouver, British Columbia, for a 14-day series of meetings in four cities with over 70,000 people attending, where

90% of the audience had never seen a miracle. In January, they held revivals in Miami and Pensacola, Florida, and in the spring, they began a huge campaign in Kansas City where they were visited by a young *Oral Roberts* just launching out on his own ministry. Branham's simple authority over sickness and demons made a life-long impression upon Oral Roberts and the young missionary *T.L. Osbourne*. Soon exhausted and ill with overwork, Branham took a five-month break; he returned to put together a team and, with *Moore,* Lindsay, Baxter, and Bosworth, went to Houston where their meetings drew up to 8,000 in a single service. During this series, the famous "halo" photograph was taken (a ring of light above Branham's head, a miniature prototype of the one supposedly seen in the sky and recorded during Kathryn Kuhlman's ministry in the San Francisco Hilton Hotel). It at least convinced the two professional photographers who shot the pictures of the reality of the supernatural; all but that one photo of Branham turned out blank upon development!

In 1950, Billy Branham went to Europe; 7,000 people filled Finland's largest auditorium night after night, with hundreds, sometimes even thousands, standing outside. He filled the largest stadiums and meeting halls in the world. In 1952, he went to Africa; in 1955, he returned to Europe, and his healing power became a worldwide legend. The younger deliverance evangelists viewed him as a man set apart, like Moses; "He was number one," said Richard Hall, "of the common run of evangelists that we have now, put twenty of them at one end and William Branham on the other; he would out-weigh them all" (Harrell, *All Things Are Possible,* p. 37). The two strange signs (some later believed them to be more spiritualistic than spiritual) he had of "vibrations" in his left hand and the amazing "word of knowledge" gift nevertheless amazed tens of thousands. Bosworth wrote in 1950: "Brother Branham is the most sensitive person to the presence and working of the Holy Spirit and to spiritual realities of any person I have ever seen. . . . when the afflicting spirit comes into contact with the gift it sets up such a physical commotion that it becomes visible. . . and so real it will stop his wrist watch instantly . . . like taking a live wire with too much current in it. When the oppressing spirit is cast out in Jesus' name, (his) red and swollen hand returns to its normal condition" (Bosworth, "Voice Of Healing," March, 1950, p. 10).

Harrell also recounts: "The Angel told him (Branham) that the anointing would cause him to see and enable to tell the suffering many of the events of their lives from childhood down to the present time. . . the great audience hears all this over the P.A. system. Brother Branham actually sees it enacted and pushing the microphone away so the audience won't hear it, he tells the patient any unconfessed and unforsaked sins in their lives which must be given up before the gift will operate for their deliverance. As soon as such persons acknowledge and promise to forsake their sin. . . their healing often comes in a moment before Brother Branham has time to pray for them" (Harrell, *All Things Are Possible,* pp.

37-38). The gift, which many insisted was "exactly 100 per cent," made him more than a channel for the gift of healing; He was a "seer as the Old Testament prophets." A interpreter for him in Switzerland and later an historian said, "I am not aware of any case in which he was mistaken in the often detailed statements he made" (Harrell, *All Things Are Possible,* p. 38). A contemporary evangelist recalled, "I've been with him when he would meet a person he had never seen and immediately call him by name" (Harrell, *All Things Are Possible,* p. 38).

Leonard Ravenhill, the evangelical revivalist and friend of A. W. Tozer, was invited as a well-known speaker. Already in the area and with a night off, he was able to fill in for a tired Branham one night during a campaign. He recalls how Branham, arriving to speak after all, another hour and a half after Len's own long message, called for "the first twenty people up here" that God would heal. After his usual public identification of the attractive young woman first in the prayer line giving her name and city through the microphone, he spoke quietly and privately to her; God would heal her if she gave up her adultery. Indignantly the man behind her protested; he was her husband, he said, and Branham had no right to say that! Turning to him in terrible quietness, Branham replied, "And God will heal you when you stop running around with your secretary." Then, speaking again through the microphone, he gave a thirty-minute gentle but searing rebuke to the audience, warning them that God's love would reveal every secret sin that stood in the way of their wholeness with Him. Returning to the prayer line, he found that every single person had left!

People came many times just out of curiosity; he preached and prayed for the sick three or four hours to exhaustion until carried bodily off the platform. There were no "hard cases" for him; in one 1950 meeting "nine deaf mutes came in the prayer line and all nine were healed" (Bosworth, "Voice Of Healing," January, 1950, p. 5). Most impressive was his quiet mastery of audiences; he "seldom raised his voice or got excited or disturbed" (Harrell, *All Things Are Possible,* p. 38). His sermons were largely stories of personal experiences, and he had a trait which impressed his audiences and colleagues alike, an "outstandingly humble spirit." "There is nothing boisterous or arrogant about him," wrote an observer, "he is a meek and humble man . . . loved by all. No one begrudges him success or is envious of his great popularity" (Harrell, A*ll Things Are Possible,* p. 39). This humility and a refusal to discuss controversial doctrinal matters won him wide Pentecostal support through the 1950's.

During this time, Oral Roberts took up the torch and led the way for others like *Jack Coe,* and *A. A. Allen,* who took to the big tents. T. L. Osbourne began to take a healing and deliverance message to the mission-field; *Tommy Hicks* went to Argentina in 1954 with reportedly as many as 400,000 persons attending a single service.

By 1955, William Branham's finances had faltered through his own carelessness, and, by 1958, he was deeply re-assessing his ministry. In the new decade, his problems seemed to intensify. By 1960, he began to stray doctrinally, embracing a *"oneness position."* [1] By 1963, he had received a "Spirit of Elijah" revelation, demanding abandonment of denomination and loyalty to this "coming messenger." On December 18, 1965, driving to Arizona, he was hit head-on by a drunken driver and died Christmas Eve.

If ever a movement was a costly, consuming blaze, this one was. "It was an exhausting, draining way of life: William Branham was a broken man after little more than a year; Jack Coe was physically exhausted at the time of his death; A.A. Allen, an incredibly tough campaigner, tottered constantly on the brink of psychological collapse; the resilience of Oral Roberts became a legend among his peers" (Harrell, *All Things Are Possible,* p. 6).

Misunderstood and caricatured by the press, disparaged by the medical profession, repudiated by most other Christian groups, and finally ostracized even by the major Pentecostal churches, the independent evangelists came face to face with seemingly insurmountable obstacles. By 1957, nearly all recognized that what had begun in 1947 was over. But, there were new opportunities in 1958—thousands in traditional churches had become interested in the charismatic message; hundreds of thousands of religious Americans were dissatisfied with their own lethargic denominations and searching for a more

[1] Oneness position: A group of people who believe that the Trinity is a single entity that is called by three different names. They reject the unity of the Father, Son, and Holy Spirit as three persons in one Godhead.

dynamic experience. As the charismatic renewal blossomed, many of these second-wave healing evangelists turned their works into missionary ministries. Consciously or unconsciously adapted to the traditional church's blossoming interest, most evangelists became teachers more than healers and recast their revival teams into teaching organizations.

Harrel notes, "Even the recent tent campaigners could not recapture the uniform and spontaneous miles of the early meetings. . . . In general, the campaigns became more stereotyped, more staged, more professional. . .the revival moved into Hilton Hotels and ornate churches, revival services were replaced by charismatic conferences and seminars" (Harrell, *All Things Are Possible*, p. 9). The time for the Third Wave had come.

PART VII

The Third Wave

1967-1975

THE THIRD WAVE

In April 8, 1966 the Time Magazine cover was—
"Is God Dead?" The 1960's counter-culture flowered
out of the compost-heap of what some called the
"post-Christian era" with a deadly vengeance; 1966-
67 introduced Timothy Leary, Ken Kesey, Haight
Ashbury, free love, and acid rock. By 1969, there
was *Woodstock*, the peak of the flower child movement and the musical event of the decade; by 1971,
the tragedy of Kent State. Then it soured. In Oakland, California, Hells Angels stage guards mur-
dered one of the *Altamont* festival fans while Mick
Jagger of the Stones cavorted about on stage in front
of the violence singing "Sympathy For the Devil."
Time was ripe for a reaction to the age's utterly
abandoned immorality; into this vacuum swept
widespread awakenings affecting both the streets,
and traditional evangelical as well as mainline
denominations. They were respectively, the *Jesus*
and the *Charismatic* Movements and *Church Renewal*.

THE JESUS MOVEMENT

Suddenly they were everywhere. Until the Jesus Movement, everyone in America knew what a Christian looked like; a white, Anglo-Saxon, Protestant, Republican cheerleader or football player, crew-cut, white shirt, and tie. Then the oddest looking people began to speak in the strangest places about the ultimately-avoided subject—Jesus. Rejecting a caricature of Christianity which had estranged them from more orthodox avenues of faith, the new converts simply called themselves "Jesus People." Full of zeal, often with strange ideas and interpretations, not always all of unquestionable purity or orthodoxy, they nevertheless exploded across the nation, forcing most of the traditional churches to either re-examine their approaches or to react in horror. *The Jesus Movement could never, in the full sense, be termed a revival.* But, it laid the groundwork, and contributed toward a wave of fresh life that, purified and trained, set the stage for what may well happen in our present generation.

Some of those early radical pioneers are now considered today's young orthodoxy; blue jeans were exchanged for three-piece suits and street preaching out of a van for T.V. programs and fundraising seminars. Nevertheless, some of the best of the Jesus Movement survived its traumatic years, and now hold either key leadership positions of ministry or are still vitally active in expanded forms of their original ministries. Those who were there in the early years will remember some of these names:

Jesus Papers: There were several key publishers of the street papers of those days. The most predominate was Duane Pederson, founder of the *"Hollywood Free Paper."* Competing with the *"Los Angeles Free Press,"* (top circ. 90,000 mark) the first issue of the *"Free Paper"* was 10,000 and grew to over 150,000 within two years. Over 200,000 of a special edition were distributed at the Rose Parade in 1971. The *"Oracle,"* a top San Francisco hip paper had an international circulation of nearly 100,000; its editor-publisher David Abraham, 23, professed conversion in 1970 and re-issued it in 1971 as a Christian paper. Carl Park's *"Truth"* (Oct. 1970) merged with Linda Meissner's *"Agape"* for a combined circulation of over 100,000. Jack Sparks (Christian World Liberation Front/Campus Crusade 1969) published *"Right On!"* (later *Radix*) in an attempt to deal with urgent social and moral issues in an intelligent way. It grew from its first issue in July 1, 1969 of 20,000 to 100,000; special issues averaging 65,000. Jack also published a modern translation of the Gospels and Epistles, and a later book on the cults.

There were the *street ministries and coffeehouses. Arthur Blessit* of Sunset Strip launched out in 1967 with seventeen other kids from five churches in his "Love-Inn" at Griffith Park, Los Angeles.

213

Then, he began the coffee-bar "His Place" in 1968 on the Sunset Strip. In two years, some 10,000 decisions for Christ were recorded (an average of a dozen a night, but up to 500 kids attended an evening). Arthur (a Baptist who later symbolically ran for president in the late 1970's) and his family continue their ministry at the hot-spots of the world carrying a large custom-made cross as a testimony to the saving power of Christ, and recently have seen miracles of healing in answer to prayer in nations like the Philippines.

Some worked with Third World young people in radical movements as well as organized street gangs —men like *Harold Brinkely* and *Ralph Garcia* of "Youth For Truth" in Sacramento, California (1967), an outreach to groups like the Black Panthers. Other converts like *Tom Skinner* (ex-member of the Harlem Lords) and *Nicky Cruz* (converted under Dave Wilkerson's ministry in New York) went on to develop national evangelistic crusade ministries.

There were early attempts at *Christian communes* like *Dick Key's* "Clayton House" in San Francisco, 1967. But, perhaps the best known survivor of those days developed out of the "House of Miracles" first in Corona and later in Costa Mesa, California. Under the leadership of the Four-square pastor *Chuck Smith* and *Lonnie Frisbee,* his first street-redeemed assistant, Calvary Chapel was established after some rocky early attempts in 1969. In 1970 alone, 4,000 prayed to "receive Christ," with over 2,000 baptized in the Pacific Ocean; Chuck's church received much media attention, and has continued to branch off into other Calvary Chapels headed up by young ministries affected by the work.

Moishe Rosen and Jews For Jesus (founded in 1970, in New York and San Francisco) continue to aggressively evangelize both Jews and Gentiles, despite lawsuits from Jewish groups. They have worked hard in both street and literature evangelism.

David Wilkerson, the Assembly Of God minister who received a call from God to the gangs and addicts of New York City, has perhaps had more influence than any other single figure in bridging the gap between orthodox Pentecostals, new charismatics, and the disenchanted street youth. His 1963 book, *The Cross and The Switchblade*, was the single most influential book of both movements; and Teen Challenge, the most powerful work of its decade. David's ministry continues in a prophetic national call to revival, and, with his son, Gary, a return to the streets.

Then there was the visionary Baptist, *Bill Bright*, with his "Campus Crusade." Called of God in 1951 in his last semester at Fuller Theological Seminary, Bright began his work with youth on college campuses. He relocated his headquarters in Arrowhead Springs, California, in 1963 with a staff of 125, and by 1972 he had a staff of over 1,000 young people with two-thirds out in the field. His vision then was of a staff of 10,000 by 1975, to influence by then 5,000,000 young Christians. They in turn, in a year, would influence 50,000,000. After a number of popular media events like Explo '72 and "I Found It," Bill has reached out to work with groups like *America For Jesus* in an attempt to give direction and leadership to the new generation of young Christians. Co-workers like *Josh McDowell* have had wide influence in international university campuses and have contributed some excellent and intellectual Christian books, such as *Evidence That Demands A Verdict*.

Hal Lindsay's The Late Great Planet Earth was the best-selling book of the decade. Lindsay believes the decade entering maturity at the time of the Second Coming was born in the few years after the creation of Israel in 1948. (That places the end-time happenings around 1990, give or take a few years.) In apocalyptic times, this intense look at the fate of the earth influenced many to reconsider the Christian claim to truth.

By December, 1969, the *Time* Cover was "Is God Coming Back To Life?"

There were, of course, some inevitable doctrinal and moral digressions of varied consequence along the way, along with some sad losses of those who had earlier been leaders in their areas.

Tony and Sue Alamo, Victor Paul Wierville, Linda Meissner (the Jesus People Army with early membership of 5,000), David Berg (1967-68 "Teens For Christ" which became in 1970 "The Children of God"), David Hoyt (Atlanta Jesus People) were all deeply involved in attempts to minister to the counter-culture. (For some, practical problems like hurt, rejection, and bitterness were never resolved. Others fell victim to deception as a consequence of confusing individual vision with an independent spirit. Some just got discouraged along the way and reacted tragically.)

Events like Sun Myung Moon's attempt to infiltrate government, media publicity over charges of brainwashing, kidnapping, and deprogramming, prominent warnings in airports, and the Manson and Jonestown tragedies created strong public reaction against early successes in Christian recruitment. But, there was more to come.

THE CHARISMATIC RENEWAL

Without a word of greeting, *Smith-Wigglesworth* strode into the office of *David DuPlessis* and unloaded to that startled Assembly Of God executive what was to prove a significant prophetic word —that he henceforth would go around the world helping spread the good news of restoration of spiritual gifts and power to Christians of all persuasions and backgrounds. Wigglesworth then abruptly left, apologetically returning moments later to offer belated greetings and introductions. Events like this were common in the early days of that spiritual outpouring of the early 1960's which ultimately involved millions of people in a fresh attempt to see the prophecy of Joel fulfilled "In the last days I will pour out My Spirit upon all flesh" (Joel 2:28).

A "new wave" in the 1960's was the Charismatic Movement, a neo-Pentecostal awakening "as remarkable as its predecessor." Charismatic clinics and Full Gospel Businessmen's conventions listed names like *Derek Prince* (Pentecostal Assemblies of Canada), *Kenneth Hagin* (raised Baptist, became Assembly Of God in 1938), *John Osteen* (Southern Baptist), *Gerald Derstine* (Mennonite), and *Bob Mumford* (Elim Bible Institute Professor of Bible and Missions). David Harrell says, "The force of the new revival astonished American religious leaders"

(Harrell, *All Things Are Possible,* p. 136). It began to be called a "Third Force" in Christendom and was made the subject of a special article in the *Encyclopedia Brittanica. Rex Humbard* and *Kathryn Kuhlman* (Evangelical Alliance), highly successful independents who never associated themselves with the earlier healing revival, were thrust into a position of leadership and honor. Rex built a T.V. ministry around his Akron, Ohio, "Cathedral of Tomorrow" church, and Kathryn packed them in each month in the Los Angeles Shrine, Pittsburgh churches, and other huge auditoriums with astonishing demonstrations of the healing power of God.

Gordon Lindsay had an aristocrat's bloodline in the healing movement; born in Zion City in 1906, he was influenced by John G. Lake in Portland in 1920 and converted under Charles Parman's ministry. With Lakes' help, he began his travels as an evangelist at the age of 18, and continued in the ministry for 18 years, first alone, and, later with his family, conducting over 150 campaigns. Work with the Assemblies Of God, a short time in the Four-Square, and many friends in other Pentecostal groups, "prepared him as perhaps no other to establish communication with a variety of Pentecostals." When World War II began, he stopped traveling, took a church in Ashlan, Oregon, and later joined William Branham.

In April of 1948, Lindsay began the *Voice of Healing* magazine; when Branham retired, leaving him to work with other young evangelists, he invested his savings to continue it. Reaching 30,000 per month the first year, it was a phenomenal success. In 1949, Gordon arranged the first convention of healing revivalists in Dallas, Texas; the following year (except for Roberts and Branham) virtually every important healing evangelist in the nation met in Kansas City. Through the 1950's, Lindsay held workshops and attempted to avert clashes between these and established Pentecostal churches. His overview of the movement was without equal. He died on April 1, 1973, the historian and theologian of the movement, leaving to his wife, *Frieda*—who successfully continued the vision—daughter, and sons: a native church ministry funding, by 1973, over 3,000 overseas church building programs in over 83 nations; a native literary work which distributed over 15 million books including more than 200 of Gordon's own titles in 46 languages; Shira (Carol) his vivacious daughter's Jewish mission in Israel; C.F.N. (Christ For The Nations), and a prayer/tape ministry sending out some 2,000 teaching cassettes a month.

Full Gospel Businessman's Fellowship: Founded in 1952 by *Demos Shakarian,* a friend and disciple of Charles Price and an organizer of Oral Roberts' 1951 Los Angeles campaign, F.G.B.M.F.I. showed the great appeal of the charismatic message outside organized Pentecostal circles. By the mid-60's, it had established 300 chapters with approximately 100,000 members. By the early 1970's, *Voice* magazine had a circulation of over 250,000. In 1972, Shakarian reported a membership of 300,000 and an annual operating budget of more than $1,000,000. It was accepted by thousands of successful middle-class people and grew explosively.

Despite tremendous growth, there was real need for *wisdom;* talented teachers began to replace gifted preachers and healers. Some of the earlier revivalists adapted to meet the challenge: Oral Roberts joined the Methodists, founded a university; Gordon Lindsay started *Christ For The Nations,* a school drawing some 1,000 international students. And T L. Osbourne established a world missionary organization specializing in native evangelism. All appealed to both mainline Pentecostals and charismatics. Many new independent evangelistic ministries flourished. Some, like David Wilkerson, had Pentecostal backgrounds; many were "Spirit-filled" ministers from traditional churches who brought teaching skills and theological training not always evident in the healing revival. Other Assembly Of God ministers like *Morris Cerullo,* a Jewish Christian, who showed "unusual ability to blend healing revivalism and charismatic teaching" and *Jimmy Swaggert* (piano-playing, singing and preaching relative of the rock pioneer Jerry Lee Lewis) became ministry bridges from the healing revival of the 1960's to the 1970's. They helped create cooperation among oldline Pentecostals, and (especially so for Cerullo) "succeeded in attracting support from the religiously dispossessed classic pentecostals and neo-pentecostals" (Harrell, *All Things Are Possible,* p. 137). Many evangelicals, caught somewhat unprepared, either experientially or theologically, to either denounce or embrace the best of the movement, have since remained at a wary distance. Others, in various attempts to constructively (or otherwise) criticize what is perceived as either unscriptural or unnecessary, have issued some form of standard public denial. Most of this is mild today. Early editions of books on the cults often associate the "Tongues Movement" with Jehovah's Witnesses and Mormons. At least one major denomination in a small nation purchased full-page ad space in a national newspaper warning about Pentecostal "demon-possession," and felt constrained to call a public meeting for their denomination. Their exhibit? A life-size photographic blow-up of a famous evangelical arm-in-arm with a well-known pentecostal during the dedication of his College with the solemn words "See? He has joined the ranks of the anti-Christ!"

Certainly, some aspects of the Charismatic Movement earned deserved and valid criticism. In some areas, there was much zeal, little knowledge, few scholarly defenders, and no shortage of power-or-money-hungry charlatans to exploit what was going on. Some non-participating fundamentalists and evangelicals traded horror stories of reported moral and religious excess in the movement; others reacted with disdain or suspicion if not downright hostility. Fortunately, today these disclaimers are made in a somewhat guarded fashion. Since the cutting edge of many awakenings around the world have involved exactly the same experiences, and simple people, unspoiled by theological prejudices, are happily repeating various aspects of the book of Acts, it is difficult to make any blanket denials lest one be found to fight against God. Now that we have had the opportunity to observe similar occurrences during the work of revivals in other nations largely cut off from the West's particular idiosyncrasies, it takes a brave soul to categorically deny all that happened in this movement as a "work of the flesh," "deception," or worse. The verdict of history is that, for millions, God spoke to them during this outpouring and used it to bring genuine life, joy, and a heartfelt desire for godly experience and truth.

One of the most controversial aspects of the Charismatic movement (at least to those Protestants who still jealously nursed what was obtained through great cost by the Reformation), is the *Catholic Charismatic Renewal*. If Baptists "speaking in tongues" is a hard enough pill to swallow, what would a theologian in the Reform tradition make of a nun or priest who does the same thing? To many Protestants, this was the final evidence of the anti-Christ; if God was going to work miracles among Catholics, He would at least first make them Protestant! Old flames here have by no means died down, even after almost two decades. Most charismatic Protestants who are unable to deny the reality of a Catholic brother or sister's walk with God simply content themselves in the wisdom and sovereignty of God; that "errors of doctrine" (as in Protestantism), are more easily corrected when one meets the Lord and has some living experience of the Truth other than that of a learned theological tradition.

Ralph Keifer was a key figure among the first Catholic Pentecostals. In Pittsburgh, Pennsylvania, in 1967, a retreat he headed broke out in charismatic manifestations which later spread to Notre Dame. The first annual Catholic Conference held at South Bend, Indiana, drew 100 people; in 1970, nearly 1,300; the next summer, approximately 5,000 registrants and 500 gate-crashers turned up, and the movement mushroomed to an estimated 50,000 people. In recent years, the proliferation of home study groups and non-Catholic doctrinal or authority-structure leanings of many of those involved has drawn some official disapproval, and in some cases active suppression by the Jesuits. But, the movement continues to expand and grow all around the world, especially in Latin American nations, where the bulk of the population are at least nominally Catholic.

David Harrell notes the shift in evangelical opinion: "Once scorned by most of the nation's religious leaders and the press, by the 1970's, Oral Roberts had become a man of prestige and stature. In 1974, David DuPlessis was included in the list of the eleven most influential Christians in the world based on an informal poll conducted by seven major church magazines. Kathryn Kuhlman's ministry was both successful and respectable. Full Gospel Businessmen's meetings took the charismatic message into the banquet halls of the best hotels in the world and boasted as members some of the world's wealthiest, most glamorous and powerful...." (Harrell, *All Things Are Possible,* pp. 4-5).

And how did the earlier Pentecostals view this new wave? Some, themselves just beginning to enjoy a new acceptance or at least a diminished criticism from other evangelicals, found themselves in the odd position of not being able to really side with it. Many retained a respectful but reluctant new denominational distance. Others, who had earlier learned the hard way the value of continued flexibility in the things of God, adapted well. Typical of these successful bridgers was Gordon Lindsay who, Harrell says, "more than any other man brought system and unity...contributing an orderly mind, keen business sense, boundless energy, badly needed literary skills and an ecumenical spirit" (Harrell, *All Things Are Possible,* p. 53).

Because God raised godly servants, a multitude of people were converted during the Charismatic Movement. Lives were changed despite human shortcomings. As Harrell notes: "Once an object of derision, by the 1970's pentecostal religion became almost fashionable. Many judged it the most vital force in American religion. By 1975 around 5,000,000 or more Americans were taking part in the charismatic revival" (Harrell, *All Things Are Possible,* p. 3).

Much attention has already been paid to figures in the early Charismatic Movement in other works, many of whom, like *Harold Bredesen, John and Elizabeth Sherrill, Dennis Bennet,* and *Ralph Wilkerson,* still continue to influence many today. Like the Jesus Movement, the Charismatic Movement had its glaring weaknesses, and drew a sometimes just share of both criticism and detractors. But, it did one thing; it broke down some barriers that had choked and embarrassed evangelicals, and compelled an entire re-examination of the work and ministry of the Holy Spirit. Without question, the movement recaptured the interest of hundreds of thousands in spiritual things, led to many conversions and miracles as people of traditional and orthodox evangelical backgrounds were forced to re-examine their faith in the light of these unusual experiences. Another neglected benefit of the renewal was the renewed hunger for teaching that, more than any other factor of the seventies, led to its great proliferation of books, audio and video cassette taped lectures, and the "seminar" approach to Christian instruction. Its strength was its emphasis on a direct, immediate, and personal experience with God and with the power of His Spirit; its weakness was at first a zeal without knowledge, and more recently, a knowledge without zeal. It was a groundwork, an opening door, a preparatory step. Above all, it left the West with a challenge to see "much greater things than these" in what may well be the Last Great Awakening.

THE CHURCH RENEWAL MOVEMENT

Since much of this movement was parallel to the Charismatic Movement, but more of an attempt to integrate into rather than come out of the mainline churches, we will not spend much time here examining some of the differences. Names like *Jack Hayford*, pastor of the Church On The Way in Van Nuys California, *Larry Christenson* of Minneapolis and *Dennis Bennett* of Seattle stand out as pastors who have worked to bring renewal within their denominational structure. Others like Derek Prince, Bob Mumford, and Charles Simpson, with national recognition as teachers and interpreters of the movement, attempted to see some sort of unity and leadership established across the charismatic renewal. They have had some limited success, though not without misunderstanding, opposition, and excesses. Men like *Ralph Wilkerson* in Anaheim, *Jerry Cook* in Oregon, and *Gerry Fry* of San Jose pioneered renewal churches modeled on both lessons learned and teachings developed from the needs of the young adults saved during those decades.

And, what of the current possibilities in modern ministries? New groups and ministries born out of the 1970's Jesus Movement and young converts of these previous two decades, with a hunger to transcend what they perceive as sub-standard levels of consecration and committment in much of our evangelical witness, today are gearing up for significant impact. Here are a few among the many who have already had a major voice among the young church of the 1980's:

Tony Salerno, like Wesley, was converted while in the ministry. Burdened for the young in both the church and the inner city, he took a small team of young converts to minister in Reedley, California, at the invitation of a godly ex-missionary pastor who for years had prayed for revival. A genuine outpouring of the Holy Spirit resulted, with the small town being deeply affected, many converted (including Barry McGuire), and the establishment of the *Agape Force.* Modeled after early Salvation Army structure and vision, the Agape Force, through traveling groups like Candle, Silverwind, Street Light, and their international "Field Stations," have had profound influence in contemporary music, children's records, and street ministry.

Bob Weiner is the founder of *Marantha Ministries,* a fast-growing confrontive and charismatic outreach among university students. Founding campus churches by open-air preaching, prayer for the sick, a strong emphasis on Christ's Lordship, holy living, and intensive discipleship, Marantha Ministries' vision for the campuses of the world make them good contenders as modern-day "Pentecostal Methodists" of the 1980's.

Jesus People U.S.A. is an example of the cream of the Jesus Movement surviving and flourishing into the 1980's. Stressing community, practical involvement with the poor and underprivileged, and a simple, radiant life style, this Chicago-based work has remained consistent to the Gospel in their communications. Resurrection Band (a band to wake the "dead") is one of the leading early "Jesus Rock" groups, and "Cornerstone" their full-color, intelligent, contemporary magazine is perhaps the best and most influential of all Jesus Papers.

Some ministries, like *Gathering Of Believers* in Washington D.C., under the leadership of influential young ministers like *Larry Tomczak, C.J. Mahaney,* and *Che Ahn,* establishing communities of practical care and help for their neighborhood areas, are now branching out to minister among the foreign language groups and refugees in large cities. *Doug Coe,* also in Washington D.C., and others of the "Brothers" on Capitol Hill work (low-profile and largely behind the scenes) to deeply affect and influence many high-level government leaders for Christ, like *Chuck Colson.* These "Brothers" work among the government personnel by friendship evangelism, and encourage events like the *National Prayer Breakfast* in the United States and other nations. *Larry Murphy*, a young American active in the early seventies in drug rehabilitation in Viet Nam, and on the Presidential Commission of Drug Abuse, is typical of those who have taken up the torch for the vast numbers of the ghetto. These sub-cultures actually have their own languages, customs, and internal coherence, as though they were small island nations among the big-city population groups.

Mario Murillo is another key voice calling for change on the West Coast and other parts of the nation. Gifted with great communicative skills, a prophet's burden, and street wisdom, he founded *Resurrection City* in Berkeley during the late 1960's, and was a key instrument in bringing a Gospel of repentance, faith, and healing back to a new generation. A Mexican-American with a torch for the disfranchized young, he has consistently shown creative, although sometimes controversial, impact as an iconoclast of current issues of contemporary idolatry. In 1982, in the midst of great personal conflict and trial, Mario saw a great outpouring of the Holy Spirit begin in San Jose, California. His vision to eventually see the whole Bay Area deeply affected by the Gospel has since spread to other states.

Keith Green, the zealous young founder of *Last Day Ministries,* did more for God in eight years than many have done in a lifetime. His newsletters, pointedly convicting songs, and concerts deeply influenced musicians and new Christians across the country. His ministry contributed toward a restoration of old principles set in new vocabulary, as well as a fearless attack on modern-day areas of sin and compromise in the world and the church. Keith Green was killed on July 27, 1982, in a tragic small plane accident with some visiting friends, his pilot, and two of his children. But, "Last Days," under the direction of his wife and co-founder *Melody,* continues Keith's work with a new emphasis on missions, care for the poor, and the publishing of reprints concerning revivals.

Perhaps one of the most significant new forces for international missions among young people is the work of *Youth With A Mission,* founded by *Loren Cunningham*, which now mobilizes thousands of young people in a variety of capacities for short-term missionary service around the world. It is currently the largest evangelical, interdenominational youth missionary movement in the world. Among some of their top leaders and directors are men like *Don Stephens* with an international rescue and training ship, *Anastasis, Floyd McClung* and his *"Dilaram"* work among the counter-culture and street people of Holland, and *John Dawson* working with groups like *Centrum* in Hollywood that specialize in reaching, among others, the victims of child pornography.

A second major work of international significance in missions is *Operation Mobilization,* founded by the fiery and intense *George Verwer,* a convert of an early Billy Graham crusade. Growing out of his missionary work in Mexico during Bible-school student days, Verwer's low-profile O.M. has established a solid, interdenominational and challenging work specializing in literature ministry through the medium of two large internationally-traveling ships, the *Logos* and the *Doulos*. George's burden is the unreached peoples of the world, especially in India and among the Muslim population. Operation Mobilization's work among these totally unevangelized may one day be recorded in history as just as significant a contribution in modern missions as William Carey's was in the past.

Some of the long-established groups like *Campus Life*, working with high school young people, have had recent fresh infusions of zealous new leadership. Men like *Doug Burleigh* of Seattle, and *Bob Krulish* of Oregon represent quality attempts to vitalize well-established *Young Life* chapters in the west and mid-western states of the nation. A growing front of dedicated young Gospel artists and musicians, who look on their talents and gifts as ministries first, have had a steady impact in Jesus Festivals and concerts across the nation since the late 1970's. There is, too, the wide influence of *Bill Gothard* whose *Institutes Of Youth Conflict* mushroomed into crowds of 20,000 or more for practical seminars on principles of Christian living, and who has had a profound influence in the evangelical consciousness of the nation.

Media influence: Touching the inner sanctum of the home via television, that great molder (and often perverter) of public opinion, some far-sighted Christians launched out to capture a section of this giant platform with a voice for God. *Pat Robertson* and *Ben Kinchlow* of *Christian Broadcasting Network (C.B.N.), Jim and Tammy Bakker* of *People That Love (P.T.L.),* and *Paul and Jan Crouch* of *Trinity Broadcasting* are the best known among the charismatics, and have established their own networks. *Jerry Falwell, Rex Humbard, Robert Schuller, Jimmy Swaggart,* and *Oral Roberts* also maintain a major exposure to the nation and overseas through their "video churches." In recent years, other faces, both new and old, male and female, have appeared in regular slots on both cable and other network programs, offering a varied bill of fare aimed mostly at Christians, with some creative programming recently geared toward housewives and children. Their alternate perspective in news events and ability to inform and nationally mobilize Christians in key issues have been a powerful influence, especially that of both Jerry Falwell and C.B.N. There is some question as to whether the two-dimensionality of television with its intrinsic tendency common to media to make people *hearers* and not *doers* of the Word, can ever trigger revival. But, if one ever happens, the channels to make such an event known are already in place, and millions can be affected in minutes.

John Giminez, ex-"Addicts For Christ" convert from New York and now pastor of the *Rock Church* in Virginia Beach, deserves mention for his visionary effort to make public America's need for change and return to Christ. His attempts to bring charismatic and evangelical leadership across the nation closer together, and for public affirmation of faith and repentance birthed the rallies called *"America For Jesus."* The Jesus Festivals are an ongoing series of gatherings under various names across the country. Initiated in 1972 in Pennsylvania (where one drew almost 70,000 during the Bicentennial Year), some like *Fishnet, Creation* and various *Jesus* regionals regularly draw accumulated attendances of 20-35,000 from all denominations. Besides offering opportunities for artists, musicians, and singers, they have become a major platform for Christian challenge, teaching, and for both evangelism and missionary recruitment.

Hope, indeed, for the nation. With all these, it is too early yet to tell what God can and may do with those who remain faithful to their calling and to their convictions. But, one thing is sure, a new breed has arisen in the ranks, "satisfied with an unsatisfied satisfaction," hungry to see something holy happen, and with them comes a genuine glimmer of light.

PART VIII

Where Do We Stand?

SIN IN THE NATION

The Current Darkness

From John Price's challenging study of the economic and political situation of the United States, *America At The Crossroads,* comes some shocking statistics. The question "Do we need a revival?" in the light of these kind of facts is pointless. Much more to the point is this question, "Do we really *want* a revival?" Sometimes God has to let really bad things happen before we realize just how much we have left His loving laws. It has been so in many of the major revivals of the past, this "darkness before the dawn"; it takes no scholar to realize that, in the Western world, it is dark enough now.

Crime: One out of every four Americans will be a victim of a "Type One Crime," a serious offence against property, or a personal or potential injury such as assault, robbery, rape, burglary, or murder. *"America is the most crime-ridden society in the world;* no other country is even close" (James Kilpatrick, "Nation's Business," April, 1975). If there are four members of your family, statistics say one of them will be the victim of a crime of violence. There is a murder every 27 minutes; 54 lives taken each day, 20,000 a year. In the 1972 Supreme Court decision (Furman vs Georgia) the death penalty was voted a "cruel and unusual punishment." When this decision was handed down, 631 were on death row awaiting execution; many of them had been waiting years. Compare this with the number of people actually killed by murder each year—20,000.

Every seven seconds a larceny is committed. Every ten seconds a burglar plys his trade. Every 78 seconds someone is robbed. A rape takes place every eight minutes. "Americans had $4.6 billion dollars of property stolen in 1977 alone. Crime is increasing because it is successful. There is only one arrest in every five reported crimes. A crook has a better than 80% chance of escaping arrest. If he does get caught, he stands a good chance of not serving time. *The Gallup Poll* says 45% of all Americans are afraid to walk in their neighborhoods at night, up from 31% in 1968. Almost 20% say they are fearful in their homes at night. The "U.S. News & World Report," September 29, 1975, observed, "Religion and morals made up 30% of the educational content of school readers prior to 1775. By 1926 religious and moral teaching made up only 6%, and has since dropped to almost immeasurable."

Abortion: On January 22, 1973, the Supreme Court decreed that unborn children had no "right to life." This decision was made in spite of the fact that the 14th Amendment of the Constitution provides that "no state...shall deprive any person of life, liberty, or property without due process of law; nor deny to any person within its jurisdiction the equal protection of the laws." Since then, over *one million* babies are killed each year, (presently closer to one and a half million), an estimated 10 million total by 1983. In Los Angeles, February, 1982, a 20x8x8 metal trash container was discovered, filled with the horrifying spectacle of numerous dead and decaying little bodies, each four pounds or more, pickled in formaldehyde and stacked in leaking tubs like ice cream containers. A week later, authorities removed hundreds more, many with perfectly formed faces and limbs, from the home of the man who once owned the now defunct medical lab that had dumped its grisly stock. As well as can be determined, a total of 17,000 fetuses, in various stages of development, were discovered. County officials would not permit news and T.V. photographers near the scene; it shocked many as badly as the news of the Nazi holocaust. *But, we are in a holocaust.* Satan must be afraid of what is coming in our generation; as he has done twice before in Biblical history, in the days of Moses and Jesus, he has a contract on the children of our time. The nation that was horrified by the cyanide deaths of Jonestown, and more recently, poisoned Tylenol, hardly seems to be bothered that more little people are killed in the United States annually by abortion than the total combined populations of Miami, Kansas City, and Minneapolis. To get around the Constitutional protection, the Court defines babies as "non-persons" even though the Constitution does not define persons. It invented a new right, "the right of privacy," based on concern for the mother. It said, "Maternity of additional offspring may force on a mother a distressful life and future. Psychological harm may be imminent, mental and physical wealth may be taxed by child care. There is also the distress for all concerned, associated with the unwanted child." William Buckley, Jr., has stated that, based on this reasoning, the whole of the adolescent class should be eliminated!

Once before in history the Supreme Court tried to usurp God's authority on human lives; in 1857, just before the great revival, the court determined the free descendents of slaves could not be citizens and that slaves were not persons (the Dred Scott case).

We must remember that Hitler didn't start by killing Jews; he began with the mentally retarded on September 1, 1939, in a private letter to two German doctors authorizing them to give incurable patients a "mercy death." Next, he killed those in retarded children's hospitals and homes; criminals in Nazi prisons; and finally, he emptied old peoples homes. Over 40,000 people were killed by Hitler before he began his anti-semite campaign. If the state can arbitrarily kill any of us who do not deserve to die, it can kill all of us. Here is a list of American war dead:

Revolutionary War - 25,324
Civil War - 498,332
World War I - 116,710
World War II - 407,316
Korean War - 54,546
Viet Nam War - 58,095

War on the UNBORN - 9,500,000 (January 1972 to January 1983).

(Barbara Syska Research Analyst, *National*

Right To Life Committee, 419 Seventh St. N.W. Suite 102, Wash. D.C. 20004.)

Legalized Wrong: Francis Schaeffer and *John Whitehead* are two nationally-known figures attempting to alert the nation to its critical situation in the law-courts of the land, particularly in regard to recent cases pending Supreme Court decisions. Some of these cases mentioned are...ministers being held liable for counseling malpractice; Christian teachers in public schools meeting for prayer; HEW requiring Bible colleges to admit drug addicts and drunks as "handicapped people"; churches forbidden to build a religious school or day-care center in areas zoned as residential; parents prosecuted for sending children to religious schools not approved by a state board of education; and pastors arrested for operating a church school not approved by the State. Secular humanism, as typified by the actions of groups like the American Civil Liberties Union, has deeply influenced the decisions of the Supreme Court and brought the country to a place Whitehead feels may trigger a "Second American Revolution." (See Schaeffer's *A Christian Manifesto* and Whitehead's *The Second American Revolution*.)

Economics: In 1929, just before the stock market crash, personal debt had risen to 88% of personal income. In 1950 personal debt was 50%. In 1974 it was 75% and has risen steadily ever since. An average of 200,000 businesses file bankruptcies every year. Of the ten largest business bankruptcies, excluding banks, in the 200-year history of the U.S.A., *five* have occurred since 1975. The three largest bank failures in 200 years happened since October, 1973—the *U.S. National Bank*, (San Diego, CA) with assets of $1,300,000,000, October, 1973; *Franklin National* (New York, NY) October, 1974, assets $3,700,000,000; *Hamilton National* (Chatanooga, TN) February, 1976, assets $450,000,000. In 1960, U.S. banks had liabilities only 11 times their capital; for every $10 in liabilities, banks had 90 cents capital, a fairly safe margin. In 1973, it was down to almost 17 times capital, or only 58 cents in $10. Some of the biggest financial institutions, like *Bank of America,* had only 33 cents for each $10. If banks collapse now they would not close as in the past, but be taken over by the Government (Emergency Banking Act of 1961).

Inflation: "Exceeding 10% a year is called 'ruinflation' because it ruins an economy and ultimately destroys a people. That kind of inflation after World War I led to the election of Hitler. In 1919 right after the war, prices rose by 50%; by 1920 were up 500% and by 1922-1923, the last year of inflation, prices increased by 14,000%! By then an egg in Germany cost 80 billion marks, a loaf of bread 200 billion marks. Reischmark notes were issued in 100 and 200 million denominations; one lady taking a wash basket of money to a bakery to buy a loaf of bread found a thief had stolen the basket and dumped the money on the ground." (John Price, *America At The Crossroads*).

There is no human solution in sight. As the Second Law of Thermodynamics points out, you can't get order in a system without a prior ordering energy and intelligence of a greater magnitude than the system needing help. As David said long ago, "It is time for Thee, Lord, to work: for thcy have made void Thy law" (Psalm 119:126).

THIRD WORLD AWAKENINGS

We come to the latter half of the twentieth century, and a brief overview of God's move among major non-Western people. Strangely enough, much of the explosive growth and national awakenings amongst the Church worldwide are taking place here.

AFRICA has given us men of the caliber of Bishop Festevo Kivengere as well as the new young prophets like the Masai evangelist, Manasseh Mankeleiyo of Kenya. In the Africa of the 1900's, one out of 13,000 were Christians; now, one out of three are reported as being Christians! Africa has experienced many powerful revivals, typical of the Belgian Congo outpouring on C.T. Studds' 1914 missionfield. "The whole place was charged as if with an electric current. Men were falling, jumping, laughing, crying, singing, confessing and some shaking terribly. It was a terrible sight. . . .This particular one can best be described as a spiritual tornado. People were literally flung to the floor or over the forms, yet no-one was hurt. (Later in the week) As I led in prayer the Spirit came down in mighty power sweeping the congregation. My whole body literally trembled with the power. We saw a marvelous sight, people literally filled and drunk with the Spirit"

(*This Is That,* pp. 12-15).

Many of these African revivals are marked by supernatural manifestations, visions, prophecies, healings, etc., and have deeply affected many parts of the Continent. Some estimates project at the present rate of growth that by the year 2,000, 50% of Africa will be converted. (So what about the "heathen in Africa?") For 35 years, there has been continuous revival in *East Africa* in countries like Kenya, Tanzinia, even Uganda under an Idi Amin! With 700 new churches in Kenya in 1980 alone, more than two new churches a day, national leaders like President Moi were praying God would make them President of the first fully Christian nation! The African Indigenous Church movement recorded over a million converts in 1970; the African revivals are powerful examples of simple faith in a miracle-working God. And, amidst sometimes terrifying persecution and political instability, they are a real testimony to the West of love under suffering.

KOREA leads the world in large churches, especially the near-legendary *Paul Yonggi Cho* with the *Full Gospel Church* in Seoul with his "Fourth Dimension" vision, prayer, and bold trust in God. Around 20% of South Korea is now estimated as being Christian; Seoul alone has 2,000 churches. Pastor Cho's Full Gospel Church, by March 31, 1982, had 250,000 members, and seats 32,000. Prayer Mountain maintains a 24-hour prayer meeting, and a new facility was built in December 1982 for seating 10,000. This powerful ministry now works with over 220 on pastoral staff; earlier they had 17 senior pastors, 45 elders, 282 senior deacons, 3,468 regular deacons, 5,000 home meetings, three services a Sunday plus afternoon worship with between 50,000 and 60,000 in each service! By 1985, Cho's church alone intends to put 10,000 new missionaries on the field; the total missionary population of both Canada and the United States around the world is 55,000. Billy Graham ministered to a crowd of 1,150,000 in Yoido Plaza in 1973; the 1980 "Here's Life Korea" crusade drew 2,700,000, the largest single preaching crowd in history with a combined attendance in four days of over 16.5 million.

CHINA has had a number of gracious visitations of God. *Jonathan Goforth,* inspired by the Welsh Revival, reports from Korea, and deeply challenged by Finney's writings, was determined to know the laws of revival and obey them. In the aftermath of strife, bitterness, and hatred that followed the massacres of the Boxer Rebellion, the young doctor challenged the divided missionaries with prayer and confession of sin. Missionaries and Chinese leaders from twenty-one stations were desperate for God; one woman leader said to Goforth, "We have prayed dry for revival here. If God doesn't send revival this time I don't see how it will be possible for us to continue in prayer. We have exhausted every prayer promise in His Book" (Rosalind Goforth, *Goforth Of China,* p. 186). Goforth had only four days; beginning with an account of an earlier revival in Manchuria, he led the people in prayer where general brokenness and confession of sin commenced. "Mr. Goforth's message was 'Not by might, nor by power, but by My Spirit,'" said one missionary. "The Cross burns like a living fire in the heart of every address. What oppresses the thought of the penitent is not any thought of future punishment but... of their unfaithfulness, of ingratitude to the Lord who has redeemed them, the heinous sin of trampling on His love... it has pricked them to the heart, moved them to the very depths of their moral being, and caused multitudes, no longer able to contain themselves, to break out into the cry, 'God be merciful to me a sinner!'" (Goforth, *Goforth Of China*, pp. 186-187). From leaders to Bible school students, and then on to the general population in different provinces, the ensuing revival touched whole communities, deeply cleansed and strengthened the church, and reached thousands for Christ.

Today, ministries like *Paul Kauffman's World Outreach* in Hong Kong have produced much literature and prayer for Communist China, laying with other intercessors a strong foundation for what God is now doing there. In 1930, missionaries felt "The doors to China are closing" and for thirty years they apparently did. Mao's revolution, however, did five things that only helped the future spread of the Gospel—he simplified language, built roads, installed communication systems, taught people to read and write in one dialect, and finally removed ancestor worship and every trace of religion! Now, into the spiritual vacuum left by his death, Christ is dealing again with this vast continent of the highest population group in humanity. There are over 50,000 house churches, with six to thirty people in each, most under 35 years old. *The Three Self* move-ment estimates anywhere between 10-20 million believers out of a population of 960 million in China. Since January, 1980, over 350,000 Bibles have been mailed in, 200,000 more in inland regions. Last year in "Operation Pearl," nearly 80% of a million Bibles were successfully distributed; brought in at night by sea, boats were met by so many Chinese Christians (in numbers estimated between five and twenty thousand believers) that the alerted local army believed it was a revolution.

LATIN AMERICA continues to grow explo-sively. In 1900, there were approximately 50,000 evangelicals in Latin America; in 1930, over a mil-lion; in 1940, two million; in 1950, five million; in 1960, ten million, and in 1970, twenty million (Peter Wagner, "Look Out! The Pentecostals Are Com-ing"). David Barrett records that of Brazil's 99 mil-lion Catholics, 60 million are involved to some degree in spiritism and 11.4 million are actually Protestants! Americans like *"Hermano Pablo" (Paul Finkenbinder)*, who labored to creatively evangelize through the media, and men like *Juan Carlos Ortiz* and *Edward Miller,* inheritors of the Argentinian awakening during the visit of *Tommy Hicks,* have done much to make known what God has done in this continent.

INDIA, that spiritually-sensitive and troubled land, has had much spiritual investment from the days of the shoemaker *William Carey* through *R.J. Ward* (Britain), praying *John Hyde* (U.S.A.) 1897, and *Amy Carmichael* (Ulster) 1906. Intelligent

Western missionaries like *E. Stanley Jones* were given doors to very high levels of government and leadership in the early 1940's. Later, healing evangelists like T.L. Osbourne ministered to large crowds with simple demonstrations of God's present power to save and deliver. Today, the practical Christian care and compassion shown by the Nobel-Prizewinning Albanian nun *Mother Teresa* and her Assembly Of God missionary friend in Calcutta, *Mark Buntain,* is a constant testimony to the reality of Jesus' love. A number of young evangelists from the West have seen large responses, in recent years, during mass crusades for evangelism coupled with prayer for the sick.

THE COMMUNIST WORLD: Here growth continues chiefly among the evangelicals, Baptists and Pentecostals providing much key leadership and life. There are now 640 registered Pentecostal churches alone in the U.S.S.R. with many more unregistered, and 250 new Pentecostal churches opening in the past five years. Though 137 million Soviets claim to be unreligious, an impressive 97 million claim to be Christians. Poland reported recently that some 30,000 young Christians meet together to seek God for the power of the Holy Spirit. Men like *Brother Andrew* and *Richard Wurmbrand* have helped the West become aware of the Underground church; books like *God's Smuggler, Underground Saints, Tortured For His Faith,* and *Vanya* have helped convey the reality of the spiritual battle. Yet, amidst the persecution and suffering, there is a reality and a hunger for God

249

often missing in the West.

All around the world, there are impressive signs of God's work, especially in the Third World and some Communist nations. But, there remains much to be done, especially among the unreached lands, the "forbidden countries" (where to become a Christian carries an automatic death sentence), and the Muslim people of the world. Asia still represents the great final continent of origins in which, by the justice of God, the "chain of Christianity," moving from there Westward over the centuries, ought to find its completion. The task is by no means nearly done. Yet, it has been frequently stated that more people will give their lives to Christ during this century than all previous centuries put together, and much of that will take place during this decade. As we leave this brief overview of the so-called Second and Third World peoples, we all ought to be haunted by an embarassing statistic: *seven thousand, six hundred people* in the West *give up* professing faith in Christ *every day*. Allowing that many are nominal Christians, allowing that some never understood the Gospel in the first place, allowing any and all other factors we can assign to justify this tragic fact, this truth remains: With all our heritage, opportunity, Scripture, and teaching, we in the West must be held deeply responsible for our hard-heartedness and apathy. True, we are seeing the fruit of God's continuous renewing and purging work; but oh, we still need a great revival. In the light of all God's work in history, our final call is to one last awakening, one that sparks our massive volume of lapsed or professed Christians into complete consecration to the living Christ and a rebirth of genuine care and compassion for others. *Shall we pray then, believe then, for the Last Wave?*

THE LAST WAVE

Ezekiel hangs over a valley. Is it a dream, a vision, or reality? At this point, he may not know and hardly cares; far below him is an open graveyard. For all he knows, it may be a prophet's graveyard who failed some ultimate test. And then the question comes to him on the wind, "Son of man, can these bones live?"

Ezekiel's chapter 37 vision is a fascinating *parallel* to what has happened in the last two decades: first, the lonely, individual prophet preaching to a hopelessly decayed situation; then, the Word creating a miracle first of reconstruction; and last, with the Wind, a military resurrection.

The Radical Sixties

If we had any word to put on the turbulent Sixties, it would have to be *"radical"*—radical politics, radical movements, "free" speech, radical "new products," technologies, radical everything. It was surely so in the Church, as shockwaves from the Jesus, Charismatic, and Church Renewal Movements interlaced and interfaced with the craziness of the streets and general culture. Yet, in these radical Sixties, with death all around, the bones began to come together.

First came the darkness. Out of a first-generation ancestry based on mere legal memory of old morality and a second generation parental license of new immorality, another generation was the counter-culture of the Sixties. Three of their characteristics were, as Charles Reich pointed out in his *Greening Of America:*

(1) *Individualism:* Of the counter-culture's three commandments, the first undoubtably was "to be true to yourself." "Doing your own thing" was "in" and conformity to anything was out. Independence became the virtue of the hour, borrowed (minus morals) from their Pioneer conscious grandparents; technology was their servant borrowed (minus status-serving trappings) from their jet-set organizational parents.

(2) *Existentialism:* How do you react to a materialistic, rationalistic and mechanistic view of the universe given by the "facts" of a Neo-Darwinian world-view? Some kids hung up "facts" all together. They saw it like this: "If the facts don't match what I know to be true by life and experience, then maybe there is something wrong with thinking. Why don't I just hang up my mind all together?" Like the smoker who read somewhere that cigarette smoking causes cancer—he decided to do something about it; he gave up *reading.* Experience-centeredness, and the idea of "nowness"—that the past or future is unimportant—gave us a generation with characteristics like these:

"They were long-haired and young and wore wild, brightly coloured clothes. Sometimes they frollicked nude in the streets, chanted obscenities at their elders and consumed generous amounts of dope ....They were protesting the materialism of their parents' generation."

Sound familiar? But they weren't hippies. They were the Bouzigos, a remarkably similar French youth movement in the 1830's. Similar movements have occurred throughout history, during the fall of Rome, the French Revolution, and the Napoleonic wars. William Moore, researcher of this article, said: "The belief in the inevitability of the future serves as a gyroscope to stabilize behavior. The loss of a future makes...an immersion in sensory experience a necessary adjustment" ("California Health Magazine").

And just like on the street, in the Church it was a decade of experience. Churches asked if you had experienced renewal. Charismatics asked if you had experienced the baptism of the Holy Spirit. The Jesus People asked if you had had an experience with Jesus.

(3) *Independent*: Most hurtful of all factors in the Sixties affecting both the Church and the streets was a terrible spirit of selfish *independence*. People did their own thing so much that their thing wound up doing them. Some church renewers told other families how to stick together when their own families were falling apart. Some charismatics believed in miracles but also got into trouble with money and immorality. Jesus People talked about "turning on to Jesus," but some still turned on with substances the real Bible Jesus definitely did not approve of.

254

The image of the Sixties was the Lone Ranger Prophet, independent from anyone, preaching to a congregation of the dead.

The Therapeutic Seventies

If the Sixties were for *radicalism,* the Seventies were for *recovery.* During the Seventies, people tried to get over the hurt they got by being radical in the Sixties. As Tom Skinner said, "Yesterday's radical is today's conservative—he's so busy trying to conserve the things he got by being radical he can't afford to be radical anymore." In contrast to the violent Sixties, the Seventies were "mellow and laid-back"; the mood was conservative, apathetic, and non-violent. The East had come to the Western culture with a vengeance and the "peace bomb" of Eastern philosophies had exploded. Terrible things were still happening in the world and neither national nor international conditions markedly improved, but no one wanted to get involved. The Sixties hurt too much; in reaction to the bitterness of that decade, the culture went about patching up her wounds in materialism and pleasure. Rock went out and Disco came in. Tom Hayden ran for regular government, Eldridge Cleaver claimed he was now a Christian, and Jerry Rubin went into the stock market.

By this time, people had begun to realize that we were living (in William Buckminster Fuller's words) on "Spaceship Earth." The limits of resources, the dangers of pollution, and nuclear escalation all promoted disagreement, an unaffordable luxury. The culture moved from radical to conformist, from individualistic to group-think, and from independent to communal. Kids switched from drugs to drink; Travolta and Winkler took fans back to the innocent Fifties with "Happy Days" and "Grease." It was time again to forget the gutsy honesty and ragged emotions of the Sixties and return to fantasy.

The awful question came to Ezekiel. Was this the test of presumption or unbelief? Was this the thing God had asked of the disconnected former citizens far below him? "And He said to me, Son of man, can these bones live? And I answered, Oh Lord God, Thou knowest. Again He said unto me, Prophesy upon these bones and say unto them, O ye dry bones, hear the word of the Lord....so I prophesied as I was commanded: and as I prophesied, there was a noise, and behold a shaking, and the bones came together, bone to his bone" (Ezekiel 37:3-7).

What did God do in the Seventies in His Church? Like the world around her, the Church moved to *community concern.* Teaching seminars, Bible studies, and tapes (both video and audio) became the new emphasis. And from the emphasis on experience (which had revived the Mystical tradition), she moved back to scripture and content, reviving the contribution of the Reformation stream.

"Is this Renewal scriptural?" the question was asked. "Do these baptisms and miracles match the Word of God?" the Charismatic Movement was queried. "Is the Jesus you experienced the Jesus of the Bible?" was the question put to the survivors of the Jesus Movement. Churches with regular, consistent Bible expositions grew by leaps and bounds; the thrust of the Church Renewal Movement mellowed, the Charismatic Movement matured into discipling, and the Jesus Movement became the new young orthodoxy.

In the Seventies, the Church set about patching up her wounds and getting her act cleaned up. The home, the family, marriage, and child-raising all came under examination. Issues like divorce, discipleship, and demons were debated. Stress was laid on the neccesity and unity for revival, cults proliferated and government reacted with broad suspicion; the Church felt the chill and the members drew a little closer to one another.

And so, the Body came together as Ezekiel watched, bone to his bone, flesh on flesh, still dead, but together. There was a great lifeless army in the valley, covered, looking definitely more promising, but without breath.

What were the sins of the Seventies? Apathy, materialism, sloth, pride. As Ezekiel put it "pride, fulness of bread, and abundance of idleness was in her and in her daughters, neither did she strengthen the hand of the poor and needy" (16:49). The Church became introspective, then self-serving. The blessing of God in financial prosperity was misinterpreted as a personal benefit, and on the eve of financial disaster and terrible social need in the culture, the Church built imposing structures as monuments to her

. vanity.

The Militant, Apocalyptic Eighties

And, so, with the invasion of Afghanistan, war in the Persian Gulf, and Ronald Reagan as President of the United States, the Eighties came. What are the marks of this decade which by all accounts is the scariest, and yet most exciting, time to be alive in all of history?

"Then He said to me, Prophesy unto the wind, prophesy, son of man, and say to the wind, Thus saith the Lord God; Come from the four winds, O breath, and breathe upon these slain, that they may live. So I prophesied as He commanded me, and the breath came into them, and they lived, and stood upon their feet, an exceeding great army" (Ezekiel 37:9-10).

God has written across the Eighties—*militancy*. And what is going on in the world is a shadow, a reflection, of what He intends to do with His Church. We have forgotten the martial music in the Church of the living God. We have forgotten that the Church is to be an "army terrible with banners," not an army that is just plain terrible. We have given much attention to the building and almost none to the battle. The note of war has been absent for a long time. But, these things will change. God has ways of getting our attention.

One thing certain about apathy is that if you do not forsake it, it will forsake you. Things get so bad that something must be done. At the end of the

Seventies, the cultural mood suddenly changed, leaving political strategies based on the liberal Seventies high and dry. New levels of stress, discontent, fear, and apparent helplessness and inability all combined to give new light to old values. The country, much to the dismay of the liberals, swung for a moment toward conservatism. Still dead, but with a national hunger to somehow put it together and to live again, they forged ahead.

The Revival To Come

And so here we are, left on the brink of the cliff like Ezekiel, listening for the sound of the wind. Do not think God has yet done all He intends to do. Revival is an act of mercy, and if ever the West needed mercy she needs it now. God has too much of an investment in the West to easily hand her over to the Destroyer; He has yet a destiny for her to fulfill. "I sought for a man," He speaks again to our times, "to stand in the gap." Can He find him in our generation?

As the world mobilizes for war, so His Church must be awakened again. A battle for world dominion is joined, and the devil does not believe in Salt Treaties with the sons of light. We—you and I—stand at the brink of the *Last Wave*. Can we venture a prophecy? He will "finish the work and cut it short in righteousness; some thirtyfold, some sixtyfold, some a hundred." The last shall be first and the first shall be last. He will sum up all He has ever done in history again. He will raise up works to illustrate His past glory. He will give to a generation, which arose without a vision or a record of His mighty works, one last chance to arise and join them. *And, you and I, living on the edge of eternity, have the fearful privilege of being a part of it. My brother, my sister—shall we go?*

PART IX

Revival Features And Impacts

FEATURES AND IMPACTS

Revivals are dangerous. They are fatal to the kingdom of darkness. They are like a temporary transfer of humanity to heaven; a transient glimpse of what it is like living in the manifest glory of God. But, few realize the cost such a divine visitation exacts from *humanity.* Mortal bodies were never designed for a continuous revival; Enoch, Elijah, and Moses, who all spent inordinate amounts of time with God, were each taken home by Him! By definition, revival cannot be other than occasional: "And the people served the Lord all the days of Joshua, and all the days of the elders that outlived Joshua, *who had seen all the great works of the Lord,* that He did for Israel...and there arose another generation after them, which knew not the Lord, nor yet the works which He had done for Israel" (Judges 2:7,10). Besides, God the Father will never spoil His children, and to live on such special visitations would be spiritually unhealthy. "Nevertheless—there is nothing more calculated to stay the rot, wean the heart from earth and attract it to heaven, and produce spiritual steadfastness than to experience such a mighty work of God. One recalls D.M. Panton's pithy definition of revival as the 'inrush of the Spirit into a body that threatens to become a corpse!' It is after all a sound military principle that the best method of defence (*sic*) is attack" (Wallis, *In The Day Of Thy Power,* p. 46).

The Steel Punch

Revival is a divine attack on society. Ever see a karate champion break a stack of bricks with his hand or a straw driven into a piece of hardwood by the violence of a tornado? Immense power concentrated in one small spot creates breakthroughs previously thought to be impossible. Israel's recapture of the Golan Heights from an entrenched Syria is a classic example of a modern military victory. Barred from the Syrian army, which was dug into three consecutive trenches in the top of the hill, by over a million planted landmines, Israeli farmers drove tractors in a straight line up the side of the hill while their Air Force strafted the enemy trenches to minimize Syrian troop groundfire. Directly behind each exploded tractor, there was another one to take its place, ploughing the ruins out of the way. The tractors, along with the Israeli troops which followed, were able to cut a straight, single line up the side of the hill which Russian advisors had assured the Syrians was unassailable. They called it "The Steel Punch," and Israel took the Golan Heights.

Wallis notes that this is the well-known military principle known as *concentration of force,* "a commander husbands his reserves, concentrates them at a strategic point for a vital blow at the crucial moment. A powerful thrust like this may accomplish what routine patrolling, skirmishing or harassing tactics could never effect." He likens this to an ancient reservoir fed by a mountain stream supplying a village community with water. One day, the wall collapses, and the waters root up large trees, carry boulders like playthings, and destroy houses and bridges and all that lies in their path. "What had before been ignored or taken for granted, now becomes an object of awe, wonder and fear. People from far and near who never went near, now hurry to see this great sight. In picture language this is revival; in fact it is the sort of picture language that Scripture uses to convey the irresistable power of God. Often in the period just preceding the movement, the stream of power and blessing has been unusually low. The people of God and work of God have been 'in great affliction and reproach' despised or ignored by those around them. In response to the burdened prayer of a remnant, God has been quietly heaping the flood. 'So shall they fear the name of the Lord from the west and His glory from the rising of the sun; for He shall come as a rushing stream, which the breath of the Lord driveth' " (Isaiah 59:19) (Wallis, *In The Day of Thy Power,* pp. 45-58).

Purpose Of Revival

Arthur Wallis was mightily used of the Lord to further the work of the Holy Spirit toward revival, especially in New Zealand. His classic study on revival, *In The Day Of Thy Power,* often quoted and excerpted from in sections of this study, has been recently condensed and re-issued (with additional material) under a new title *Rain From Heaven* (Bethany Press, 1981). In his section on "This Is The Purpose," Arthur further analyzes why God works in history by means of revivals. God is our Creator. So that we will not forget His reality or drift easily into a Deism, He still periodically alters human history by sudden, mighty moves of His Spirit. "The world of mankind has not advanced by evolution but revolution," said P.V. Jenness, "by violent upheavals in society. Eden, the Flood, Exodus, Captivity are Old Testament examples, Pentecost the conspicuous new. The Renaissance and Protestant Reformation in the fifteenth century changed the whole thought and life of Europe. Modern history dates from them" (Wallis, *In The Day Of Thy Power,* p. 45). The great missionary advance of the 19th century derived its momentum from the widespread revivals that blessed America and Britain during those years; much of the evangelistic explosion in many third world countries today can be directly traced to revivals. *"Revival is Divine military strategy; first to counteract spiritual decline and then to create spiritual momentum"* (Wallis, *In The Day Of Thy Power,* p. 45).

As has been said, history repeats itself. But, are there any patterns to revival? Perhaps if there are, we can learn from them. Richard Lovelace, in his contribution to historical and experiential theology of revivals, *The Dynamics of Spiritual Life,* points out that both history and Scripture show two patterns of divine intervention:

(1) *The New Testament* pattern is one of revitali-

zation of the Church, such as that treated by many historians of revival such as J. Edwin Orr, and dealt with in some detail by men like Arthur Wallis; and

(2) *The Old Testament model* of reform is one of structure and doctrines which move the Church "toward certain norms of life and health" and call out the blessings of God upon a nation (Lovelace, *The Dynamics of Spiritual Life,* p. 52).

Every new generation experiences what the 1960's called "The Generation Gap" often phrased as "God has no grandchildren." The Bible puts it like this: "All that generation were gathered unto their fathers, and there arose another generation after them, which knew not the Lord" (Judges 2:10).

We face it today, as did our spiritual fathers before us—the cycle of change and decay, of reformation and apostasy, the existence of a nation with a godly heritage that follows the pattern of Israel's four-fold collapse:

> Israel forgot GOD
> Israel forgot God's LAWS
> Israel made up NEW gods
> Israel made up NEW LAWS

The Law Of Moral Entropy

Why do nations leave the ways of God? There is, of course, an active devil; he never sleeps, knowing what can happen if people get carried away with being godly. People forget their roots, and spiritual history is no exception. But, there is another factor at work, one illustrated by the best-authenticated physical law in the universe, the Second Law of Thermodynamics. Put simply, things tend to run down, not up; move from order to chaos, from cohesive complexity to random simplicity. The Second Law means that the energy of a system is transformed into a different, less structured, type of energy. The measure of this disorder is called entropy. The Bible reveals that there has been a *moral entropy* introduced in our race by the Fall of man. Without a constant investment of higher power and ordering wisdom, man, left to himself, will decay, disorder, and die. All these add up—an active devil, a godly generations' death, and a law of internal decay. For this reason, revival is mandatory: we need continuous reform and re-awakening.

Another one of the observations of physics is the marked difference between *static and sliding friction*. An object at rest tends to remain at rest. An object in motion tends to remain in motion. Put simply, it is always harder to get something moving than to keep it moving once it has started. We have a parallel, personal responsibility to be sensitive to the Holy Spirit when He is dealing with mankind; the initial stage of a real awakening is critical. Imagine people pushing a stalled car. Initially, only one man in front pushing against them in the wrong direction can stop it cold. But, once it begins to move, heaven help anyone who gets in the way! Revival is like this. Anyone privileged to participate in the initial dealings of God must be wise enough in His ways not to grieve Him and allow the work to continue through to the moving; but once underway, it will move anything out of its path.

In Israel's time, under God's judgment, people awakened to a realization of better days and linked this back to their previous relationship with Him. Prayer went up in agony for deliverance, and God raised up another leader and another restoration. You can see it in the cyclical story of Biblical history, in the Gideons, Jepthas and Jehosaphats, the Hezekiahs and the Josiahs, where one man pleaded with God for the many, where one godly man stood up for the nation instead of a godly nation standing as one man. It is in the record of the book of Judges where those like God's "Incredible Hulk" Sampson stood in the gap for an apostacising nation like other heroes before and after him, generation after generation. It is these intercessors that we are in need of today—now—so that the Spirit of God may work mightily toward revival.

FEATURES OF REVIVAL

We have seen in the studies of the four exceptional men of the First and Second Great Awakenings some of the characteristics of the lives of revivalists; we have looked on these two centuries as illustrations of the New Testament model of revival. But, how can we summarize the dominant features of such a New Testament pattern? Charles Finney said, "The antecedents, accompaniments and results of revivals are always substantially the same as in the case of Pentecost." Arthur Wallis, keying off the Scriptural record of the second chapter of Acts, and quoting extensively from that "Prince of Revivalists" Finney, gives an outstanding outline of a true revival's characteristics, here excerpted and partly amplified:

Divine Sovereignty: Implicit in the phrase "When the day of Pentecost was fully come" (Acts 2:1), every genuine revival is clearly stamped with the hallmark of God's sovereignty. Consider the timing, the significance of the day, and the nations all divinely ordered there. "God times every outpouring, a *kairos* related to a thousand other plans He alone can coordinate. Finney, speaking of the 1857 Revival mentions this sovereignty: 'When I was in Boston...a gentleman stated he had come from

Nebraska and had found prayer meetings established throughout all the vast extent of country over which he had traveled.' Think of that— a vast region of 2,000 miles, along which the hands of the people of God were lifted up in prayer! From North to South till you come within the slave territory, a great and mighty prayer went up to God that He would come down and take the people in hand and convert souls; and He heard everybody stood astounded." Likewise in the Welsh Revival, "The outpouring of the Spirit came dramatically with precision in the second week in November 1904 on the same day —both in the north and the south."

Spiritual Preparation: The two essential conditions of revival are *unity* and *prayer*. "All together in one place. . . . with one accord continued steadfast in prayer" (Acts 1:14). Revival has two foundation stones: "the preparedness of man and the sovereignty of God" (Wallis, *In The Day Of Thy Power,* p. 60). The Word and history teach us that an attitude of indifference and fatalism must be abandoned before revival can be expected. If the blessing comes, then we may be sure someone has met the conditions and paid the price. "Yet. . . we cannot have revival as if God is at our beck and call. 'Thy people offer themselves willingly in the day of Thy power'" (Psalm 110:3; Ezekiel 36:33-37; Mark 6:5,6; Deuteronomy 11:13,16-17) (see *Spontaneous Working*).

Suddenness: "And suddenly there came. . ." (Acts 2:2). In revival, God's work may be sudden and unexpected; often even believers are caught unawares, while fear and astonishment grip unbelievers' hearts. "They would wake up all of a sudden, like a man just rubbing his eyes open and running around the room pushing things over and wondering where all this excitement came from. But though few knew it, you may be sure there had been somebody on the watchtower constant in prayer until the blessing came" (Wallis, *In The Day Of Thy Power*, p. 62). Revival is God springing a convicting surprise on His creation. "I have declared the former things from the beginning; and hear they went forth out of My mouth, and I shewed them; I did them *suddenly* and they came to pass...and new things do I declare: before they *spring forth* I tell you of them" (Isaiah 48:3; 42:9). The effect of the sudden working of the Spirit in revival is very striking in the conviction of sinners. Often without any preparatory concern or even thought for spiritual things, a sinner will be suddenly seized with overwhelming conviction of sin.

The modern horror movie shock tactic of sudden confrontation with the unexpected is a perverted, cheap copy of a holy original—the awesome fear of the Lord. Suddenness is a divine shock tactic to remind men of their spiritual vulnerableness. "But God shall shoot at them; with an arrow *suddenly* they shall be wounded...and all men shall fear; and they shall declare the work of God and shall wisely consider His doing" (Psalm 64:7,9). John Shearer, in *Old Time Revivals,* writes of a farmer returning from market in Ulster at Ballymena in 1959. "Mind wholly intent upon the day's bargain, he pauses, takes out some money and begins to count it. Suddenly an aweful (*sic*) Presence envelopes him. In a moment his only thought is that he is a sinner standing on the brink of hell. His silver is scattered, and he falls on the dust of the highway crying out for mercy" (Shearer, *Old Time Revivals,* p. 63).

Spontaneous Working: Revival is the result of divine, not human, impulse. It cannot be worked up. "There came a sound from heaven" (Acts 2:2). Fulfilled conditions do not provide the motive force of revival. Revival, like salvation and healing, is an act of divine mercy. Like salvation, too, its grounds are God's grace though its conditions are repentance and the prayer of faith. (Acts 3:19: "seasons of refreshing. . .from the presence of the Lord") "A movement bears this mark of spontaneity when men cannot account for what has taken place in terms of personalities, organizations, meetings, preachings, or any other consecrated activity; and when the work continues unabated without any human control." As soon as a movement becomes controlled or organized, it has ceased to be spontaneous—it is no longer a revival. The course of the 1904 revival has been outlined thus: "God began to work; then the Devil began to work in opposition; then God began to work all the harder; then man began to work and the revival came to an end" (Wallis, *In The Day Of Thy Power,* p. 65).

God-consciousness: The spirit of revival is the

273

consciousness of God. Men were "pricked in their heart" (Acts 3:7); "fear came on every soul" (Acts 2:43). "The effects of such manifestations of God are twofold; men are made aware both of His power and His holiness. This manifestation...was intensely personal" (Wallis, *In The Day Of Thy Power,* p. 66). It is God moving in power and holiness toward you; God coming for you, and calling your name! "Here is an outstanding feature of revival; it is easy to see why it results in overwhelming conviction both among the saved and the lost whenever there is unjudged sin....At such times man is not only conscious God is there; but that He is there, it seems, to deal with him alone, until he is oblivious of all but his own soul in the agonizing grip of a holy God." If these facts are borne in mind, the extraordinary effects of past revivals will not seem incredible.

The ruthless logic of Jonathan Edwards' famous discourse, "Sinners In The Hands Of An Angry God," could not have produced the effect it did had God not been in the midst. "When they went into the meeting house the appearance of the assembly was thoughtless and vain; the people scarcely conducted themselves with common decency," recorded Trumbull. But, he goes on to describe the effects of the sermon, "the assembly appeared bowed with an aweful (*sic*) conviction of their sin and danger. There was such a breathing of distress and weeping that the preacher was obliged to speak to the people and desire silence that he might be heard" (Wallis, *In The Day Of Thy Power,* p. 67). Conant says, "Many of the hearers were seen unconsciously holding them-

274

selves up against the pillars and the sides of the pews as though they already felt themselves sliding into the pit" (Wallis, *In The Day Of Thy Power,* p. 67). Finney, at the village schoolhouse near Antwerp, New York, describes such conviction: "An aweful (*sic*) solemnity seemed to settle upon the people; the congregation began to fall from their seats in every direction and cry for mercy. If I had a sword in each hand, I could not have cut them down as fast as they fell. I was obliged to stop preaching."

Sometimes the manifested presence of God creates a *divine "radiation zone"*; all coming within that expanding spiral of tangible power are brought under awesome conviction. During the 1857 Revival, no town in Ulster was more deeply stirred than Coleraine. A schoolboy in class became so troubled about his soul that the schoolmaster sent him home. An older boy, a Christian, went with him, and before they had gone far led him to Christ. Returning at once to school, this new convert testified to his teacher: "Oh, I am so happy! I have the Lord Jesus in my heart" (Orr, *The Second Evangelical Awakening,* p. 44). These simple words had an astonishing effect; boy after boy rose silently, left the room. Going outside, the teacher found these boys all on their knees in a row along the wall of the playground. Very soon, their silent prayer became a bitter cry; it was heard by another class inside and pierced their hearts. They fell on their knees and their cry for mercy was heard in turn by a girls' class above. In a few moments, the whole school was on their knees! Neighbors and passers-by came flocking in, and, as they crossed the threshold, they all came under the same convicting power. Every room was filled with men, women, and children seeking God.

During the same 1857 Revival in America, ships entered a definite zone of heavenly influence as they drew near port. Ship after ship arrived with the same talk of sudden conviction and conversion. A captain and an entire crew of thirty men found Christ at sea and arrived at port rejoicing. *This overwhelming sense of God bringing deep conviction of sin is perhaps the outstanding feature of true revival.* Its manifestation is not always the same. To cleansed hearts it is heaven; to convicted hearts it is hell.

Anointed Vessels: There is a fresh emphasis on the Person and work of the Holy Spirit. "They were all filled with the Holy Ghost" (Acts 2:4). "With those stirrings of the Spirit that are the precursor of revival there is born in many such hearts a wholesome dissatisfaction with that vague and mystic view of being filled with the Spirit that leaves one in the dark as to what it is, how it comes and whether or not one has received it" (Wallis, *In The Day Of Thy Power,* p. 69). Finney again says, "Many times great numbers of persons in a community will be clothed with this power, when the very atmosphere of the whole place seems to be charged with the life of God. Strangers coming into it and passing through the place will be instantly smitten with conviction of sin and in many instances converted to Christ" (Wallis, *In The Day Of Thy Power,* p. 71).

Supernatural Manifestation: The most ordinary conversion of a sinner is a supernatural work, but it is not manifestly so. Here is meant that which is in the eyes of men manifestly supernatural and which can be accounted for in no other way. "They spoke in other tongues as the Spirit gave them utterance" (Acts 2:4). It is that which produces in the hearts and minds of onlookers the reaction described here, "they were all amazed, and were perplexed saying one to another, What meaneth this?" (Acts 2:12).

Revival always seems to bring with it a return to apostolic Christianity. Never is the Church nearer to the spirit and power of the first century than in times of revival. In times of spiritual blessing, the gifts are most especially manifest. It has been so in every great revival from the days of Whitefield to Evan Roberts. Spurgeon noted, "If you read the story of the Reformation, or the later story. . . of Whitefield and Wesley, you are struck with the singular spirit that went with the preachers. The world said they were mad; the caricature drew them as being fanatical beyond all endurance; but there it was, their zeal was their power. Of course the world scoffed at that of which it was afraid. The world fears enthusiasm, the sacred enthusiasm which is kindled by the thought of the ruin of men and by the desire to pluck the firebrands from the flame, the enthusiasm which believes in the Holy Ghost, which believes God is still present with His church to do wonders" (Spurgeon, *Sermons On Revival,* p. 15).

Crying out and falling down under the Spirit was

common in the Wesley-Whitefield revivals. Lady Huntingdon wrote to Whitefield advising him not to remove those who were under the power of the Spirit as it had been done because it seemed to bring a damper on the meeting. "You are making a mistake. Don't be wiser than God. Let them cry; it will do a great deal more good than your preaching" (Wallis, *In The Day Of Thy Power,* p. 75). This seems to have been a natural reaction of people in the Scriptures who had a divine "close encounter" of the fourth kind—the invading sense of God's convicting power. Wesley recorded in his journals of July 7, 1739, "He (Whitefield) had opportunity of informing himself better; no sooner had he begun...to invite all sinners to believe in Christ than four persons sunk down close to him almost in the same moment. One of them lay without sense or motion. A second trembled exceedingly. The third had strong convulsions all over his body but made no noise unless by groans. The forth, equally convulsed, called upon God with strong cries and tears. From this time I trust we shall allow God to carry on His own work in the way that pleases Him."

Sometimes this sense of identification with the hurt of God is awesome, terrifying. An observer of the Welsh Revival, David Matthews, said of Evan Roberts, "Mr. Roberts had an experience which I believe was never repeated.... Prayer was the keynote of his tireless life. No action taken or engagement entered into was done so without definitely committing the matter to God. His soul appeared to be saturated through and through with the spirit of prayer. It was the atmosphere in which he moved and lived...whenever one looked on his face, he seemed engaged in intercession; when this incident was far in the past *he asked God to give him a taste of Gethsemane;* later in his Christian experience such a request would have been unthinkable.... However the fact remains, and I am a living witness of the incident, that the prayer was answered in a terrifying way. Falling on the floor of the pulpit he moaned like one mortally wounded, while his tears flowed incessantly. His fine physical frame shook under crushing soul-anguish. No one was allowed to touch him.... The majority of us were petrified with fear in the presence of such uncontrollable grief. What did it mean?... No one doubted the transparent sincerity of the man however mysterious the happenings. When Evan Roberts stood before the congregation again, his face seemed transfigured. It was apparent to all he had passed through an experience that was extremely costly. No one who witnessed that scene would vote for a repetition. One wonders whether such a hallowed scene should be chronicled" (Matthews, *I Saw The Welsh Revival,* p. 41).

Divine Magnetism: During the Lewis Awakening in the village of Arnol, there was no response in the first meetings; at the close of an evening meeting, a time of prayer was convened in a house. As one man was praying, all who were present became aware that the prayer was heard and that the Spirit of God was being poured out on the village. They left the house to discover the villagers also leaving their cottages and making their way as though drawn by some unseen force to one point in the village. There they assembled and waited. "And when this sound was heard, the multitude came together" (Acts 2:6). And, when Duncan Campbell commenced to preach, the word took immediate effect. In a few days, that small community had been swept by the Spirit of God and many souls truly converted. The evangelist often complains that unconverted, pleasure-loving masses will not come to hear the Gospel; that large sums are spent on publicity and advertising, and witness marches are held in the streets. But, where normal means are failing to achieve the necessary end, where natural means do not succeed, we must look to the supernatural. "How long halt ye between two opinions?" Elijah said, but "the people answered him not a word" (1 Kings 18:21). But when God answered by fire, instantly the people were on their faces. What the strivings of men cannot achieve is but the work of a moment to the outpoured Spirit.

Apostolic Preaching: Although many souls are saved in revival apart from preaching, such times are nearly always characterized by powerful proclamations of truth. "Peter lifted up his voice and spoke forth to them" (Acts 2:14). Sometimes the outpouring has come by preaching; sometimes the preaching has come by the outpouring. "There is a rugged grandeur about the apostolic preacher which recalls the fearless prophet of Old Testament days. They were clothed with the same power and impelled by the same boldness for their torches were lit from the same holy fire. . . . The primary aim is to lead souls to repentance. . . . There is so much emphasis today on believing, receiving, deciding and so on and so little on the vital step of repenting. . .the men dealt faithfully with the question of sin that the conscience might be aroused" (Wallis, *In The Day Of Thy Power,* p. 82).

"It was a precept of Wesley's to his evangelists in unfolding their message to speak first in general of the love of God to man; then with all possible energy so as to search the conscience to its depths, to preach the law of holiness; and then, and not till then, to uplift the glories of the gospel of pardon and of life. Intentionally or not, his directions follow the lines of the epistle to the Romans" (Bishop Hadley Moule on Romans). Finney had a fixed principle in dealing with souls: he would never tell a man how to get right with God until he could no longer look the man in the face.

The realm of *apostolic preaching* may be subdivided into four categories: spontaneous preaching, anointed preaching, fearless preaching, and Christ-centered preaching. All of these are vital elements in any Spirit-led revival and have been evidenced throughout history.

1. *Spontaneous preaching:* "For some twelve years," said Finney, "in my earliest ministry I wrote not a word; and was commonly obliged to preach without any preparation whatever, except what I got in prayer. Often I went into the pulpit without knowing upon what text I should speak or a word that I

should say. I depended on the occasion and the Holy Spirit to suggest the text and to open up the whole subject to my mind; and certainly in no part of my ministry have I preached with greater success or power. If I did not preach from inspiration I didn't know how I did preach. It was a common experience with me...that the subject would open up to my mind in a manner that was surprising to myself. It seemed that I could see with intuitive clearness just what I ought to say and whole platoons of thoughts, words and illustrations came to me as fast I could deliver them" (Wallis, *In The Day Of Thy Power,* p. 84).

Far from encouraging laziness, such a manner of preaching demands incessant prayerfulness and constant meditation and feeding on the Word. In the Evan Mills revival: "The Spirit of God came upon me with such power that it was like opening a battery upon them. For more than an hour the Word of God came through me to them in such a manner that I could see was carrying all before it. It was a fire and a hammer breaking the rock, and as the sword that was piercing...I saw a general conviction was spreading over the whole audience" (Wallis, *In The Day Of Thy Power,* p. 84).

2. *Anointed preaching* is "in demonstration of the Spirit and of power" so that faith does not stand "in the wisdom of men, but in the power of God" (1 Corinthians 2:1-5). One said of Savonarola, the great Italian reformer: "Nature had withheld from him almost all the gifts of the orator" yet "when we read of his intense and enrapt communion with God,

his unconquerable persistence in seeking the power of the Highest till his thoughts and affections were so absorbed in God...those who looked in his cell saw his upturned face as if it had been the face of an angel" (Wallis, *In The Day Of Thy Power,* p. 85). His preaching was so moving, melting, resistless that a reporter put down his pen with this apology written under the last line "Such sorrow and weeping came upon me that I could go no further."

3. *Fearless preaching* is the result of God's anointing. "They spoke the word of God with boldness." Of Gilbert Tennant, a contemporary of Jonathan Edwards, and mightily used in the New England Revival, it has been noted that "he seemed to have no regard to please the eyes of his hearers with agreeable gestures, nor their ears with delivery, nor their fancy with language; but to aim directly at their hearts and consciences, to lay open their ruinous delusions, show them their numerous secret, hypocritical shifts in religion and drive them out of every deceitful refuge wherein they had made themselves easy with the form of godliness without power.... His preaching was frequently both terrible and searching" (Wallis, *In The Day Of Thy Power,* p. 86). Fearless preaching is calculated to produce conviction or stir up the bitterest animosity. It usually does both.

4. *Christ-centered preaching* is the basis for all other forms of preaching. Consider the Moravian Revival. In the 30 years following the outpouring of the Spirit on the congregation at Herrnhut (1727), the Moravian evangelists, aflame for God, had car-

ried the Gospel not only to nearly every country in Europe but also to many pagan races in North and South America, Asia and Africa. Dr. Warnek, German historian of Protestant Missions, wrote, "This small church in 20 years called into being more missions than the whole evangelical church has done in two centuries" (Wallis, *In The Day Of Thy Power,* p. 88). More than one hundred missionaries went forth from this village community in 25 years. Where the Spirit of God is in control, there is an inevitable return to the simple methods of the first century, and many are surprised to discover they not only still work, but they still work the best. They are, in fact, the only channels capable of carrying the mighty rivers of blessing let loose in revival. We will see how great those rivers can be.

Superabundant Blessing: "And there were added unto them in that day about three thousand souls" (Acts 2:41). "Many that heard the word believed; and the number of men came to be about 4,000" (Acts 4:4). "And believers were the more added to the Lord, multitudes of both men and women" (Acts 5:14). "And the number of the disciples multiplied . . . exceedingly; and a great company of priests were obedient to the faith" (Acts 6:7). If the recorded results of that outpouring at Pentecost were not part of inspired Scripture, we might have wondered whether the accounts were not exaggerated. Yet, down through the years, there have been seasons of revival at least numerically comparable to Pentecost.

It is estimated that 30,000 souls were converted

through Whitefield's revivals in America. In the Second Great Awakening, Dr. Henry Ward Beecher remarked to Charles Finney, "This is the greatest revival of religion that has been since the world began" (Wallis, *In The Day Of Thy Power,* p. 90). It is computed that 100,000 were converted that year in the United States. In the great 1857 Revival, conversions numbered 50,000 a week. And, according to Finney's estimate in 1859 when the revival was still spreading over the whole United States, there could not have been less than 500,000 conversions. "In the year 1859 a similar movement began in the United Kingdom affecting every country in Ulster, Scotland, Wales, and England, adding a million accessions to the evangelical churches" (Wallis, *In The Day Of Thy Power,* p. 90). The 1904 Revival touched almost five million people in two years; the closing years of this century have witnessed even more massive ingatherings.

Far more significant to thoughtful minds than massive statistics is the proportion of a community that is affected. Of the New England Revival (18th century), Conant wrote, "It cannot be doubted that at least 50,000 souls were added to the churches of New England out of a population of about 250,000. A fact sufficient to revolutionize, as indeed it did the religious and moral character and to determine the destinies of the country" (Wallis, *In The Day Of Thy Power,* p. 90).

Of the Northampton, Massachusettes (1735) revival, Edwards wrote, "There was scarcely a single person in the town, either old or young, that was left unconcerned about the greater things of the eternal world. Those...the vainest and loosest, most disposed to think and speak lightly of vital and experimental religion, were now generally subject to great awakening. The work of conversion was carried on in an astonishing manner, and increased more and more; souls did, as it were come by flocks to Jesus Christ" (Edwards, *Works Of Jonathan Edwards*, p. 91). Finney wrote of the revival in Rome, New York, "As the work proceeded it gathered in nearly the whole population." Of the 1857 Revival in Stockholm, Sweden, he also noted, "At least 200,000 persons have been awakened out of a population not exceeding three million" (Edwards, *Works Of Jonathan Edwards*, p. 91).

Divine Simplicity: In a mighty movement of the Spirit, sometimes the link is snapped, the revival movement is severed from the old machinery, and then linked to the new which is fit to receive and use the fresh output of power. New wine requires new wine-skins, and if the old are not prepared to be renewed and remodeled by the Spirit of God to meet new situations, God has no alternative but to reject them. "As faith and spirituality decline, the power of the Spirit is gradually withdrawn. Soon it becomes necessary to substitute human arrangement worked without the Spirit's power for the divine arrangements dependent on that power.... How simple were the channels along which the rivers of that first outpouring flowed! The corporate life of the first Church was maintained by no methods or devices more complex than teaching, fellowship, breaking of bread, and prayers. The means were simple, but they were sufficient. When the Spirit of God is poured out again it will be seen that nothing more is needed" (Wallis, *In The Day of Thy Power,* pp. 94-95).

FEATURES OF REVIVALISTS

John Gillies, in his 1795 classic, *Accounts of Revivals,* noted what he perceived to be the marks of a revivalist. Here is a summary of those characteristics:

(1) They were *earnest* about the great work of the ministry on which they had entered.... They felt as ministers of the Gospel they dared not act otherwise; they dared not throw less than their whole soul into the conflict; they dared not take their ease...they dared not be indifferent to the issue when professing to lead on the hosts of the living God against the armies of the prince of darkness.

(2) They were *"bent upon success";* to be indifferent to their office would have been to "prove themselves nothing short of traitors to Him and to His cause. As warriors they set their hearts on victory and fought in faith anticipating triumph under the guidance of such a Captain."

(3) They were *men of faith.* They ploughed and sought in hope. They knew, in due season, they would reap if they did not faint. They had confidence in God, in their Savior's commission, in the promise of Scripture and the Holy Spirit's almighty power and grace.

(4) They were *men of labor.* They bore the burden and the heat of the day...freely offered to the Lord,

keeping back nothing, grudging nothing, joyfully, thankfully, surrendering all to Him who loved them. They labored for eternity as men who knew the time was short and the day of recompense was at hand.

(5) They were *men of patience*. They were not discouraged though they had to labor long without seeing all the fruit they desired. They were not soon weary in well-doing.

(6) They were men of *boldness and determination*. Enemies might oppose, timid friends might hesitate, but they pressed forward, in nothing terrified by difficulty or opposition. It requires more than natural courage to face natural danger and difficulty. There is, in our own day, a still greater need of moral boldness, in order to neutralize the fear of man, the dread of public opinion—that god of our idolatry in this last age, which boasts of superior enlightment, and which would bring everything to the test of reason or decide it by the votes of the majority.

(7) They were *men of prayer*. It is true they labored much, visited much, studied much, but they also prayed much. In this they did abound. They were much alone with God replenishing their own souls.

(8) They were *men of most decided doctrine* both in law and Gospel. There was a breadth and a power in their preaching—a glow and an energy about their thoughts and words that makes us feel they were "men of might." Their trumpet gave no feeble, uncertain sound either to saint or sinner, the church or the world.

(9) They were *men of solemn deportment and*

deep spirituality. Their daily work furnished the best illustration of what they preached. No frivolity, flippancy, worldly conviviality or companionships neutralized their public preaching or marred the work they were seeking to accomplish. They lived what they preached. (Gillies, *Historical Collections Of Accounts Of Revivals,* pp. vi-xi).

THE SOCIAL IMPACT OF REVIVALS

If one of the definitive marks of revival is its ability to change the "moral climate of a community," in what areas of society will we notice the most change? Historically, the *extremes*—the upper and lower strata of a country's educational system, economic structure, moral stance, health care facilities, and the attitudes toward age and the media—are the main areas which undergo a significant amount of change. God's work touches and transforms the outer limits of that society. True revival, then, would alter and include:

The *educational* system includes teachers and students, educators and pupils. In our day, the conflicts are over Christian verses Public schools, voluntary prayer, creationism, textbook censorship, and the teaching of the religion of secular humanism.

The *economic* structure involves wealthy and poor, business and slums. Today the call is for sweeping relief in the inner city, reassessment of presently adopted assumptions of both socialism and capitalism, waste, and the increase of major industries which are built around addictions, affluency, and joblessness.

The *moral* stance takes in the realm of the Church and the criminal, seminaries and prisons. Today, it deals, on the one hand, with both liberalism and evangelical humanism, and, on the other, with rising crime, and prison reform and rehabilitation.

Health care facilities include doctors and the sick, psychiatrists and the insane, as well as the current trends of carelessness, easternized holistic care, abusive drug, childbirth, vaccination, and surgery procedures, abortion clinics, and organ transplant and sperm bank misuse.

Media are culture definers and proliferate mass culture. Today's media problems include challenged direct mail privilege, television access by cable and satellite, anti-Christian and occultic propaganda in the arts, including film, television, theater, and the record industry.

Age conflicts affect children and infants, the elderly or retired, and involve the areas of abortion and genetic manipulation, euthenasia, retirement homes, mandatory retirement, and inadequacy in pensions and health insurance plans.

Bill Gothard points out that where the Church fails in her commission, government must assume the burden, and thus it acquires that corresponding power of influence. Instead of the early nation's strong family and church-based education, we have amoral and humanistic public schools. Instead of her ministry of care and healing, we have the clinical and costly public hospital. Instead of Christian charity, we have government welfare. Having steadily defaulted responsibility to the government in most other areas, we only seem to notice with alarm this loss when the same government begins to directly intrude on the Church herself, with taxation, zoning, and other abusive ordinances. Dorothy Sayers (Anglican theologian and friend of C. S. Lewis and J.R.R. Tolkien) noted that the poor always have to be cared for and the burden born by the more well-off, whether church or government does it. The difference is that with the true Church, support is a Gospel concern with gifts of compassion and care. With government, it is a legal issue and the money is exacted from the rich in taxes. The sad consequence is that love is thereby eliminated and replaced by law and civic duty.

Yet, in each era of revival, an awakened Church returns to shoulder its abandoned responsibility to a hurting world. Indeed, much of that which is publicly charitable and socially compassionate in society has Christian roots, like many orphanages, hospitals, rehabilitation and social centers. In 1842, Albert Barnes, friend of the revivalists in his day, author of a classic book on the atonement, and pastor for 40 years at the First Presbyterian Church in Philadelphia, said:

"One sin is interlocked with others and sustained by others...the only power in the Universe which can meet and overcome such combined evil is the power of the Spirit of God. There are evils of alliance and confederation in every city which can never be met by a general revival of religion" (Barnes, *Revivals In Towns And Small Cities,* in "The American National Preacher," XV, 1841, pp. 12-13,15).

William Arthur's book, *Tongue Of Fire,* released in half-a-dozen editions in England and America after 1854, laid out to the Methodists their duty to the inner city if they believed in deliverance from all sin and entire consecration. He warned that the two most dangerous perversions of the Gospel were to look on it as a "salvation for the soul after it leaves the body but no salvation from sin while there" and as "a means of forming a holy community in the world to come but never in this one." He also said: "Nothing short of the general renewal of society ought to satisfy any soldier of Christ...much as Satan glories in his power over an individual, how much greater must be his glorying over a nation embodying in its laws and usages disobedience to God, wrong to man and contamination to morals? To destroy all national holds of evil; to root sin out of institutions; to hold up to view the Gospel idea of a righteous nation...is one of the first duties of those whose position or mode of thought gives them any influence." In doing so, they were "at once glorifying the Redeemer" by showing how lovely His influence over society was and by removing hindrances to individual conversions, some which directly incite to vice, others that uphold a state of things which shuts God out. "Satan might be content to let Christianity turn over the subsoil (if he can continue to forever sow the surface with thorns and briars) but the Gospel is come to renew the face of the earth" (Arthur, *Tongue Of Fire,* pp. 145-146).

In the 1857 Awakening, Christian concern with poverty, the rights of women, children, and working people, the evils of the liquor traffic, slum housing, and racial bitterness blossomed into a thousand different movements and ministries to see the nation change. In England, Christians who disagreed on other areas stood together against the sin of the streets. Perhaps, divided in methods and mind-set like Shaftesbury and Booth, they were yet one in motive. Unable to let the nation alone, they fought both in government halls and on filthy streets against the abuse of working people, their children, and the poor. Briefly, here is a synopsis of the most recognized reform movements, many of which are still in active existence today in one form or another.

The Salvation Army

By all accounts, the one most obvious example of Christian social compassion and practical concern by any group in contemporary history is the Salvation Army. The works of the holy Army launched by the young Methodist *William Booth* (1829-1912) and his astonishing wife *Catherine Mumford Booth* (1820-1890) are legendary. Almost every type of outreach and care for the poor and downtrodden imaginable were both attempted and usually successfully implemented by this radical band. William's *In Darkest England And The Way Out* outlines a scheme for the rehabilitation of an entire nation, a grand social reconstruction plan a century ahead of its time. Catherine's brilliant preaching and writing affected hundreds of thousands. Her temperance tracts, written under an assumed name, were widely distributed throughout Europe. Though suffering from curvature of the spine, never to know a pain-free day in her life, and often lonely and confined, *she read the entire Bible straight through eight times by the time she was twelve years old.* Shortly after, at 14, she mastered *Finney's Systematic Theology,* along with other volumes by Butler, Fletcher, Wesley, and other holiness writers. These famous works led to her strong messages on Christian perfection which were to characterize the Army's motivation for service to the world. When Catherine died, more people attended her funeral than had the Queen of England's (10,000!). William was universally honored by statesmen and kings the world over for his work with the poor and underprivileged; 35,000 people attended his funeral. But, one of the most radical challenges the Salvation Army made to sin in society came from one of their sons, Bramwell, in a controversial media exposure that rocked a nation.

Maiden Tribute

Bramwell Booth's young and pretty wife, Florence, blue-eyed and normally serene, flinched as the full horror of the truth she had uncovered struck her sensitive spirit. Managing the "Refuge," a temporary haven for runaway girls, streetwalkers, and hookers, she was prepared for evidence of London's widespread prostitution. But, she was not prepared for what she discovered: a terrible network entrapping young girls—innocent children often younger than thirteen or fourteen. The network posed as employment agencies, condoned hideous initiations, and then shipped the young girls as human sexual slave traffic to rich debauchers throughout England and sometimes (drugged and nailed alive into coffins) to the Continent. The "age of consent" in "moral" Britain was then only *thirteen* in contrast to the Continent's twenty-one. Yet, three times legal efforts to raise this age in England were met with defeat; one policeman *wanted it lowered to ten!* London was steeped in prostitution; *one in every fifty English women were hookers,* with 80,000 prostitutes in the city and 2,000 pimps working Charing Cross alone. Their clients were "men in high places; not only members of Parliment, but Queen Victoria's cousin, the King of the Belgians who spent 1,800 pounds a year debauching English girls" (Richard Collier, *The General Next To God,* p. 111). Another lecher proudly boasted that he had "ruined 2,000 women." One home near Farnham for "fallen children" housed forty girls under twelve years of age. One at Newport, *housed fifty under ten.* "In only four instances had any of the perpetrators been punished. Two London men had outraged respectively sixteen and a dozen children, only one was convicted. The plea?—the children over thirteen had consented; and those under thirteen could not know the nature of the oath! In eight weeks no fewer than thirty cases involving injury to forty-three girls between three and thirteen years old were brought before the courts" (Madge Unsworth, *Maiden Tribute,* pp. 17-18).

With her own baby daughter beside her, thinking of other little girls' anguish and degradation, Florence cried herself to sleep night after night. Bramwell, her tenderhearted husband, was shocked but secretly doubted it could be so bad. Determined to check it out, he shortly after met a seventeen-year-old girl, Annie Swan, who had escaped during the entrapment process. Further questioning of other rescued girls confirmed the horrible truth—a slave-traffic that "could not be matched by any trade in human beings known to history." The twenty-six-year-old Salvation Army Chief Of Staff then wrote, "I resolved—and *recorded the resolve on paper* — that no matter what the consequences might be, I would do all I could to stop these abominations, to rouse public opinion, to agitate for the improvement of the law, to bring to justice the adulterers and murderers of innocence, and to make a way of escape for the victims!" (Bramwell Booth, *Echos And Memories,* p. 120).

Working with a new convert, Rebecca Jarrett, a thirty-six year old ex-drunkard and brothel-keeper for twenty years, and the famous London editor, William T. Stead, the Salvation Army launched a fantastic plot to confirm and expose the children's slave traffic—one that was eventually to embroil the Army in bitter controversy, and result not in the arrest and conviction of the child traders, but of Jarrett and Stead! Jarrett posed as a procurer and Stead as "one of the wealthy debaucherers to whom so many hundreds of the children of the poor were annually sacrificed." Obtaining a pretty child called Eliza Armstrong for two pounds from her mother, they played out and documented the entire process, releasing it in the July 6, 1885 issue of the *Pall Mall*

Gazette. It "took the British public by storm, in a way that can hardly be paralleled in newspaper history" (Unsworth, *Maiden Tribute,* p. 25). Where it was opposed, young Bernard Shaw himself offered to go out and sell the paper; where it was in demand, enterprising newsboys sold the last copies at exorbitant prices.

The "dead" Criminal Law Amendment Bill was suddenly resurrected before a packed and excited House of Parliment. Within seventeen days, *over 343,000 signatures filled the Salvation Army's "monster petition"* to the House of Commons. Two miles in length, the petition was carried by eight Salvationists onto the floor of the House. In a month, the Bill was law, and the age of consent was raised to sixteen. But the underworld, outraged at their exposure, counterattacked. They took Stead and Jarrett to court indicting them under an 1861 abduction act! This "most sensational trial of the nineteenth century" ended in Bramwell's acquittal, but Stead and Jarrett respectively received three and six month sentences. They had succeeded. It cost them all dearly, but they broke the back of one of the most vile and vicious practices in England's history.

American Reform

And what of America? Her great abomination was slavery. Africa was raped for America's prosperity, and *a total of ten million men and women were carried away. A hundred million died.* The defenders of slavery claimed it was "a Christian

299

institution," a "positive good," because "among other things it brought the heathen from Africa and gave them the elements of a Christian civilization!" The 1857 Revival was to so deeply affect the destiny of the United States that revival-created sentiments over this issue helped put Abraham Lincoln into Presidency and ultimately led to the Civil War, the most costly attempt evangelicals ever made to see righteousness applied to a nation.

Gilbert Hobbes Barnes' revolutionary study on the real roots of anti-slavery stands as one of the great historical discoveries of the movement. His eventual book flew in the face of the five major interpretations of the causes of the Civil War. The lost papers and letters he found showed the true cause of anti-slavery. He "held up the religious faith of individuals, the moral ideals of heroes, the dedicated efforts of a handful of determined men, a Holy Band, who pitted themselves against the political might, the economic power and the social folkways of a whole nation in order to stand up for what their hearts told them were eternal, universal, 'higher' spiritual laws" (Barnes, *The Anti-Slavery Impulse,* p. xix).

Can a revival message change a nation? Preaching in a day when some 50,000 conversions were taking place each week, Charles Finney and other reformers of that time period truly believed that Christ, in the lives of His holy people, was going to change the world. They had a concern for personal and social perfection, a pure zeal fired by revival, and, above all, they had a message radical enough to overthrow the entrenched religious selfishness of their times. "What made Finney an epochal figure was not his eloquence or his 'new measures'; it was the new doctrine he preached....The emotional impulse which Calvinism had concentrated on a painful quest for a safe escape from life, Finney thus turned toward benevolent activity. Converts, he declared, did not escape life; they began a new life 'in the interest of God's Kingdom.' In this new life they have 'no separate interests'....They should set out with a determination to aim at being useful in the highest degree possible. Among Finney's converts this Gospel released a mighty impulse toward social reform" (Barnes, *The Anti-Slavery Impulse,* pp. 11-13).

In Finney's "Holy Band," there were self-effacing co-workers like *Theodore and Angela Grimke Weld,* and converts to holiness like the wealthy New York Tappan brothers. The crusade against slavery was a direct result of revival convictions and conversions, "which led...to the formation of countless abolition societies, the arousing of a religious crusade against slavery which was more significant and important in the election of Lincoln and the outbreak of the Civil war" than the egocentric, pompous rhetoric of William Lloyd Garrison, the "evil genius" in the East (McLoughlin, Introduction, *The Anti-Slavery Impulse,* pp. viii).

"Abolition is essentially a revival" an anti-slavery paper explained, "a revival of the principles of liberty and social religion...the reformation was a revival of the entire system of Christianity which in

301

the lapse of centuries has been transformed into a sort of idolatry." They looked on the American Revolution as a "political revival—a new and striking exemplification of the great doctrine of human rights" and Abolitionism as a "two-fold revival (of the) law of love in relation to man," and then "of the principles of liberty, as proclaimed by our forefathers. Its necessity has arisen from the national violation of this law, a national departure from these principles" (Benjamin P. Thomas, from the Foreword, *Theodore Weld,* p. vii). Oberlin and Lane Seminaries, set up to train evangelists and revivalists, were the first two colleges to welcome black and white students, and to allow men *and* women to enter the ministry. They likewise took a terribly unpopular stand against slavery because they believed it a sin against God.

The roots of this anti-slavery revolution were first laid a century earlier by the Quaker radical, *George Fox.* In 1657, he warned against the practice of slavery based on the equality of all men in the eyes of God. Fox was no mere meditating mystic. Rufus Jones calls him ". . . a brave and heroic character, a rugged, unpolished man battling with immense difficulties and oppositions, but revealing often a fine humour, and always a large patience and a mighty faith. . . . He learned to stand in a hostile world. He managed to endure a long series of prison confinements that would have broken any constitution not well supplied with iron sinew. His journeys, when he was out of prison. . . were usually difficult and dangerous and full of exposure to the elements of nature" (Jones, *Journal Of George Fox,* p. x).

Fox's journal reads like the diary of some holy secret agent, a sacred revolutionary. Next only to his absolute certainty that he had a "direct and immediate correspondence with God" was his love for people which resulted in a declaration of spiritual war on all who hurt them. He had, perhaps better than any other of his time and nation, a "clear, sure insight into the moral and social issues of his time." Because Fox loved God, he really loved man. Jones says again, "From his own first-hand experience there emerged a profound conviction which lasted all his life that God and man are essentially related because their spiritual frontiers are continuous and undivided. There is something in man that is not of dust, or earth, or flesh or time, but of God....Fox has many ways of saying this in his seventeenth-century phrases...faith gave him an exalted sense of the infinite worth and preciousness of man, of every man, of every type and degree" (Jones, from the Preface, *Journal Of George Fox,* pp. x-xi).

Fox "put his finger with almost infallible certainty upon the sore spots and evil tendencies around him. He was as tender as a mother over all who were victims...of man's brutality, injustice, stupidity, greed or carelessness. He hated every artificial fashion which contracted the full human life of any man or woman. He went about his task of liberating men and transforming society with an absolute confidence in God's guidance and in the power of His Spirit, with an unlimited faith in human possibilities and in the effectiveness of the spirit of sincere love and kindness when put full into practice. . . .In any case, nothing has ever worked any better than this method of love and friendship, this transmission of the spirit of Christ" (Jones, *Journal Of George Fox,* p. xii).

Dumond, a major authority on anti-slavery, asserts that the early Quakers were no ignorant "obnoxious group of meddlers" any more than the later anti-slavery leaders of the nineteenth century, as was charged and commonly believed. The Quakers, too, were originally rich, powerful slaveholders, who came to their decision through a "century of soul-searching and consultation." Then they "opposed slavery from the first to the last on moral and religious grounds—as a sin. They made tremendous financial sacrifices to rid themselves of the contamination. They never asked anything for themselves by way of profit—political, social or economic—from their friendship for the oppressed. Nevertheless, they were silently denounced, charged with citing rebellion, suppressed and finally driven out of Barbados because they sought to evangelize and educate their slaves. They were denied the poor privilege of freeing their slaves in the southern states and in the early congress of the United States accused of treason and incendiarism because they petitioned for the suppression of the African slave trade" (Dumond, *Anti-Slavery—The Crusade For Freedom In America,* pp. 16-17).

Leading the early pre-Revolutionary abolitionists was the gentle New Jersey tailor, *John Woolman,* "The greatest Quaker of the eighteenth century and

304

perhaps the most Christ-like individual Quakerism has ever produced." He was accompanied by the Philadelphia schoolmaster-organizer *Anthony Benezet,* whose friendship and correspondence with John Wesley led to that Methodist's tract *"Thoughts On Slavery"* copied almost verbatim from Benezet. Woolman, Dumond says, was a "humanitarian in the finest sense of the word; he knew the truth, spoke the truth and men believed because they had no other choice. Wealth, war and slavery were to him the three greatest enemies of the souls of men" (Dumond, *Anti-Slavery—The Crusade For Freedom In America,* p. 17). When they began, 30,000 slaves died every year, bought, sold, worked, and killed like cattle. When their spiritual descendents finished, a nation had suffered the judgment of God, and they had broken the legal back of the greatest abomination of the land.

Anti-slavery in the United States, like abortion, prison reform, and other civic controversies of our day, had to be tackled head-on as a moral issue. Our times call for another restoration of that godly imperative; a *message which expects and demands practical holiness for both individual and community is the need of the hour.* We have simply ignored the essentials of true conversion; the society-affecting principles of *prayer and fasting, confession and restitution, genuine forgiveness, reproof and rebuke, care for the poor, the old, the widows and orphans, and the necessity of every-believer evangelism.* Biblical repentance is three-fold; from *idolatry* (false gods), *personal iniquity* (individual sin), and *social injustice* (corporate evil). Our modern version of "repentance" is counted as heroic if we pass stage one; counterfeit conversion is the order of the day. As Allein pointed out so long ago, we are supposed to repent not only from the world, the flesh, and allegience to the devil, but from *our own righteousness*—or in modern terms, our own *rights* or good things. Today we "suggest" an abandonment of the first three (as options for a "growing" Christian) and urge professed converts to "consecrate" their "good things." Only recently has the concern for genuine heart-purity become a watchword again in the young Church, not as an option, but as a *mandate* for the truly converted. Only in the last decade has there been a serious interest again in dealing with entrenched evil in the structures of law, medicine, government, media, and education.

Here, perhaps, is a valid contribution of the "Moral Majority." It takes no scholarship to realize that no majority of this Majority need necessarily be Christian at all; just "nice" people who want to preserve a previous lifestyle from a threatened destruction. Moral Majority people can be Protestant, Jewish, Catholic, Mormon, or Ku Klux Klan— essential evangelical experience is hardly required to feel outrage at a collapsing society which may seriously threaten your freedom, security, and peace. But, as Francis Schaeffer points out in *A Christian Manifesto*:

"... We must realize that regardless of whether we think the Moral Majority has always said the right things... they certainly have done one thing right;

they have used the freedom we still have in the political arena...they have carried the fact that law is king, law is above the lawmakers, and God is above the law into this area of life where it always should have been. The Moral Majority has drawn a line between the one total view of reality and the other total view of reality and the results this brings forth in government and law. And if you personally do not like some of the details of what they have done, do it better. But you must understand that all Christians have got to do the same kind of thing, or you are simply not showing the Lordship of Christ in the totality of life" (Schaeffer, *A Christian Manifesto,* pp. 61-62).

The Moral Majority, and like groups, represent attempts to bring society back toward these "norms of life and health." Like Josiah of old, who tore down idols and cleaned out Israel without knowing why his nation was so deeply fallen, not all have "the Book of the Law." But, God has worked through imperfect men before; God has raised up men with a little light where there has previously been no light at all in order to bring greater light.

CONCLUSION

When the question is asked: *"What hinders revival?"* one of the simple answers is this: *We do not have men and women who are prepared to pay the same price to preach the same message and have the same power as those revivalists of the past.* Without these firm believers, the community can never be changed. Our concern is concilitory, our obedience optional, our lack theologically and culturally justified. *Quite simply, it costs too much!* We say we want revival. But, who today is prepared to live a life of absolute obedience to the Holy Spirit, tackling sin in the Church as well as the street, preaching such a message of perfection of heart and holiness of life—a message feared and hated by the religious and street sinner alike? Are we prepared?

SUGGESTED READING LISTS

Works On Revival

1. *All Things Are Possible,* by David Edwin Harrell, Jr., Indiana University Press.
2. *Another Wave Of Revival,* by Frank Bartleman, Whitaker House.
3. *The Awakening That Must Come,* by Lewis A. Drummond, Broadman Press.
4. *The Dynamics Of The Spiritual Life,* by Richard Lovelace, I.V.F. Press.
5. *Evangelical Awakenings,* by J. Edwin Orr, Bethany. This is a set of five volumes, all in paperback and excellent reading. See Bibliography.
6. *The Flaming Tongue,* by J. Edwin Orr, Moody Press.
7. *The General Next To God,* by Richard Collier, Collins.
8. *The Great Awakening,* by Joseph Tracy. Out of print, but try the library.
9. *Historical Accounts Of Revivals,* by John Gillies, Banner Of Truth.
10. *Lectures On Revivals Of Religion,* by Charles G. Finney, Bethany.
11. *Personal Declension And Revival,* by Octavius Winslow, Banner Of Truth.
12. *Power From On High,* by John Greenfield. Out

of print.
13. *Power Through Prayer,* by E.M. Bounds, Baker, Whitaker House, and Zondervan.
14. *Rain From Heaven,* by Arthur Wallis, formerly entitled, *In The Day Of Thy Power,* Bethany.
15. *Reality,* by Arthur Katz, Logos.
16. *Reflections On Revival,* by Charles G. Finney, Bethany.
17. *Revival Praying,* by Leonard Ravenhill, Bethany.
18. *Revivalism And Social Reform,* by Timothy Smith, Abingdon Press
19. *Revivals Their Laws And Leaders,* by James Burns. Out of print.
20. *Why Revival Tarries,* by Leonard Ravenhill, Bethany.

Revival Biographies

1. *Aimee—Life Story,* by Aimee Semple McPherson, Foursquare Publishing.
2. *All Things Are Possible,* by David Edwin Harrell, Indiana University Press.
3. *Aspects Of Pentecostal/Charismatic Origins,* by Vincent Synan, Logos.
4. *Autobiography Of Charles Finney,* by Charles G. Finney, Bethany.
5. *Billy Graham,* by J.C. Pollock. Out of print.
6. *Christian Leaders Of The 18th Century,* by J.C. Ryle, Banner Of Truth.
7. *The General Next To God,* by Richard Collier, Collins.
8. *George Whitefield,* by Arnold Dallimore,

Banner Of Truth.

9. *Goforth Of China,* by Rosalind Goforth, Bethany.
10. *Holy Company,* by Elliot Wright, MacMillan.
11. *The Jesus Movement In America,* by Ed Ploughman, David C. Cook.
12. *Journal Of David Brainerd,* by Jonathan Edwards. Out of print.
13. *The Journal Of George Fox,* by Rev. Norman Penney, Everyman's Library.
14. *Lord Shaftesbury,* by Florence M.G. Higham. Out of print.
15. *Moody,* by J.C. Pollock, MacMillan.
16. *Shout It From The Housetops,* by Pat Robertson, Logos.
17. *Signs And Wonders,* by Maria Woodworth-Etter, Harrison House.
18. *Smith-Wigglesworth Remembered,* by William Hacking, Harrison House.
19. *Strangely Warmed,* by Garth Lean, Tyndale.
20. *Twenty Centuries Of Great Preaching,* by a collection of authors, Word.

For Further Study

1. *A Christian Manifesto,* by Francis Schaeffer, Crossway Books.
2. *America At The Crossroads,* by John Price, Tyndale.
3. *America Is Too Young To Die,* by Leonard Ravenhill, Bethany.
4. *A Time For Anger,* by Francis Schaeffer,

312

Crossway Books.

5. *Destined For The Throne,* by Paul E. Billheimer, Christian Literature Crusade.

6. *The Emerging Order,* by Jeremy Rifkin, Dutton.

7. *God's Strategy In Human History,* by Forster and Marsden, Send The Light Press.

8. *Lectures On Revivals Of Religion,* by Charles G. Finney, Bethany.

9. *Operation World,* by P.J. Johnstone, Send The Light Press.

10. *The Promise Of The Spirit,* by Charles G. Finney, Bethany.

11. *Rain From Heaven,* by Arthur Wallis, formerly entitled, *In The Day Of Thy Power,* Bethany.

12. *Reflections On Revival,* by Charles G. Finney, Bethany.

13. *Revivalism And Social Reform,* by Timothy Smith, Abingdon Press.

14. *Revival Praying,* by Leonard Ravenhill, Bethany.

15. *The Revival We Need,* by Oswald J. Smith. Out of print.

16. *The Search For America's Faith,* by George Gallup, Jr., Abingdon Press.

17. *Today's Gospel—Authentic Or Synthetic?,* by Walter Chantry, Banner Of Truth.

18. *The Truth Shall Make You Free,* by Gordon Olsen, Bible Research Fellowship.

19. *The World Christian Encyclopedia,* by David Barrett, Oxford.

20. *Youth Aflame!,* by Winkie Pratney, Bethany.

BIBLIOGRAPHY

Andrews, J.R., *The Life Of George Whitefield,* Morgan and Scott, 1879.

Bartleman, Frank, *Another Wave Of Revival,* Whitaker House, 1982.

Best, Mary Agnes, *Rebel Saints,* Harcourt Brace, 1925.

Booth, Bramwell, *Echoes And Memories,* Hodder and Stough, 1925.

Bready, J. Wesley, *This Freedom Whence,* Light and Life Publishers, 1950.

Campbell, Duncan, *God's Standard,* Christian Literature Crusade, 1967.

Collier, Richard, *The General Next To God,* Fontana/Collins, 1976.

Dallimore, Arnold, *George Whitefield,* Cornerstone Books, 1970.

Dowley, Timothy, *History Handbook Of Christianity,* Eerdmans, 1977.

——————————, *The History Of Christianity,* Eerdmans, 1977.

Drummond, Lewis, A., *The Awakening That Must Come,* Boardman Press, 1978.

Dumond, Dwight Lowell, *Anti-Slavery Crusade For Freedom,* University Of Michigan Press, 1961.

Durant, Will, *The Reformation,* Simon and Schuster, 1957.

Edman, V. Raymond, *Finney Lives On,* Bethany, 1951.

——————————, *They Found The Secret,* Zondervan, 1961.

Edwards, Jonathan, *Works Of Jonathan Edwards,* Yale University Press, 1959.

Finney, C.G., *Autobiography Of Charles Finney,* Bethany, 1979.

——————————, *Heart Of Truth,* Bethany, 1976.

——————————, *Lectures On Revival,* Bethany, 1979.

——————————, *The Promise Of The Spirit,* Bethany, 1980.

——————————, *Systematic Theology,* Bethany, 1976.

Fischer, Harold A., *Reviving Revivals,* Gospel Publishing House, 1950.

Forster and Marsden, *God's Strategy In Human History,* Tyndale, 1973.

Fox, George, *Journal Of George Fox,* Everyman's Library, 1940.

Frodesham, Stanley, *Smith-Wigglesworth, Apostle Of Faith,* Assembly Of God Publishers, 1965.

——————————, *With Signs Following,* Gospel Publishing House, 1946.

Gallup, George, Jr., *Search For America's Faith,* Abingdon Press, 1980.

Gee, Donald, *Wind And Flame,* Heath Press, 1967.

Geikie, Cunningham, *The English Reformation,* Strahan and Co., 1879.

Gillies, John, *Accounts Of Revival,* Banner Of Truth, 1981.

Goforth, Rosalind, *Goforth Of China,* Bethany, 1937.

Graham, Billy, *America's Hour Of Decision,* Van Kampen Press, 1951.

——————, *Revival In Our Time,* Van Kampen Press, 1950.

Greenfield, John, *Power From On High,* Christian Literature Crusade, 1950.

Hacking, W., *Smith-Wigglesworth Remembered,* Harrison House, 1981.

Hardesty, Nancy, *Great Women Of Faith,* Baker/Abingdon Press, 1980.

Harrell, David Edwin Jr., *All Things Are Possible,* Indiana University Press, 1975.

Harris, R. Laird, *Theological Workbook Of The Old Testament,* Moody Press, 1980.

Higham, Florence, *Lord Shaftesbury,* MacMillan, 1945.

Hobbes, Barnes Gilbert, *The Anti-Slavery Impulse,* Harbinger/Haco Press, 1933.

Hodder, Edwin, *The Life And Work Of Shaftesbury,* Cassell and Co., 1870.

Hulburt, Jesse Lyman, *The History Of The Christian Church,* Zondervan, 1970.

Lake, John G., *Adventures In God,* Harrison House, 1981.

Lean, Garth, *Brave Men Choose,* Blandford Press, 1961.

——————, *Strangely Warmed,* Tyndale, 1964.

Lindsay, Gordon, *The Gordon Lindsay Story,* Voice Of Healing, 1958.

——————, *Men Who Changed The World,*

Christ For The Nations, 1959.

Lovelace, Richard F., *The Dynamics Of Spiritual Life,* I.V.F. Press, 1980.

MacDonald, Williams, *True Discipleship,* Walterick, 1962.

Marsh, Josiah, *The Popular Life Of George Fox,* Charles Gilpin, 1847.

Matthews, David, *I Saw The Welsh Revival,* Moody Press, 1978.

McNeil, *History And Character Calvinism,* Oxford, 1954.

McPherson, Aimee Semple, *Aimee,* Foursquare Publishers, 1979.

McPherson, Anna Talbot, *They Dared To Be Different,* Moody Press, 1967.

Miller, Basil, *John Wesley,* Bethany, 1966.

Miller, R. Edward, *The Flaming Flame,* Argentine Bible, 1973.

Nixon, Leroy, *John Calvin, Expository Preacher,* Eerdmans, 1950.

Olford, Stephen F., *Lord Open The Heavens,* Harold Shaw, 1980.

Orr, J. Edwin, *Campus Aflame,* Regal, 1971.

_____, *Eager Feet,* Moody Press, 1975.

_____, *Evangelical Awakenings In Africa,* Bethany, 1975.

_____, *Evangelical Awakenings In Eastern Asia,* Bethany, 1975.

_____, *Evangelical Awakenings In Latin America,* Bethany, 1978.

_____, *Evangelical Awakenings In Southern Asia,* Bethany, 1975.

——————————, *Evangelical Awakenings In The South Seas,* Bethany, 1976.

——————————, *The Fervent Prayer,* Moody Press, 1974.

——————————, *The Flaming Tongue,* Moody Press, 1968.

——————————, *The Second Evangelical Awakening,* Marshall Morgan, 1949.

Overton, J.H., *John Wesley,* Methuen and Co., 1891.

Penn-Lewis, Jesse, *War On The Saints,* Christian Literature Crusade, 1978.

Pierson, A.T., *George Mueller Of Bristol,* James Nisbet and Co., 1899.

Pollock, J.C., *The Cambridge Seven,* I.V.F. Press, 1955.

——————————, *Moody,* MacMillan, 1963.

Price, John, *America At The Crossroads,* Living Books/Tyndale, 1976.

Quiller-Couch, A.T., *Hetty Wesley,* Morgan and Scott, 1903.

Ravenhill, Leonard, *Why Revival Tarries,* Bethany, 1978.

——————————, *Revival Praying,* Bethany, 1979.

Reich, Charles, *The Greening Of America,* Random House, 1970.

Richardson, Don, *Eternity In Their Hearts,* Regal, 1981.

Rifkin, Jeremy, *The Emerging Order,* G.P. Putnams, 1979.

Ryle, J.C., *Christian Leaders Of The 18th Century,*

Banner Of Truth, 1978.

Schaeffer, Francis A., *A Christian Manifesto,* Crossway Books, 1981.

Singer, C. Gregg, *Theological Interpretation Of American History,* The Craig Press, 1964.

Smith, Timothy L., *Revivalism And Social Reform,* Abingdon Press, 1957.

Snyder, Howard A., *The Radical Wesley,* I.V.F. Press, 1980.

Synan, Vincent, *Aspects Of Pentecostal/Charismatic Origins,* Logos, 1975.

Tari, Mel, *Like A Mighty Wind,* New Leaf Press, 1971.

Taylor, Mendell, *Exploring Evangelism,* Beacon Hill, 1964.

Thomas, Benjamin P., *Theodore Weld,* Rutgers University Press, 1950.

Unsworth, Madge, *Maiden Tribute,* Salvationism Publishing, 1949.

Various Authors, *Champions Of The Truth,* Religious Tract, 1898.

Various Contributors, *The Story Of The Welsh Revival,* Fleming H. Revell, 1905.

Walker, Williston, *A History Of The Christian Church,* T & T Clark, 1930.

Wallis, Arthur, *In The Day Of Thy Power,* Christian Literature Crusade, 1956.

Waugh, Alexander, *Biographical Sketches Of Eminent Christians,* Religious Tract, 1850.

Wesley, John, *Journals Of John Wesley,* Epworth Press, 1938.

─────────────, *Primitive Remedies,* Woodbridge

319

Press, 1973.

Williams, J.E. Hodder, *The Life Of Sir George Williams,* Hodder and Stough, 1958.

Woodworth-Etter, Maria, *Signs And Wonders,* Harrison House, 1916.

Woolsey, Andrew, *Duncan Campbell,* Hodder and Stough, 1974.

Word, *Twenty Centuries Of Great Preaching,* Word Publishers, 1978.

Wright, Elliot, *Holy Company,* MacMillan, 1980.

W.E.C., *This Is That,* Christian Literature Crusade, 1954.